Woman

Woman

The Forgotten Story

Cindy Koch

An Imprint of 1517 the Legacy Project

Woman: The Forgotten Story

Published by:
New Reformation Publications
PO Box 54032
Irvine, CA 92619-4032

Printed in the United States of America

Publisher's Cataloging-In-Publication Data
(Prepared by The Donohue Group, Inc.)

Names: Koch, Cindy.
Title: Woman : the forgotten story / by Cindy Koch.
Description: Irvine, CA : NRP Books, an imprint of New Reformation
    Publications, [2017] | Includes bibliographical references.
Identifiers: ISBN 978-1-945978-40-1 (hardcover) | ISBN 978-1-945978-41-8
    (softcover) | ISBN 978-1-945978-42-5 (ebook)
Subjects: LCSH: Women—Religious aspects—Christianity. | Women—Identity—
    Religious aspects—Christianity. | Women—History.
Classification: LCC BV639.W7 K63 2017 (print) | LCC BV639.W7 (ebook) |
    DDC 230.082—dc23

NRP Books, an imprint of New Reformation Publications is committed
to packaging and promoting the finest content for fueling a new Lutheran
Reformation. We promote the defense of the Christian faith, confessional
Lutheran theology, vocation and civil courage.

Contents

A Gift 1

Dust, Life, Death. 7

Named 15

The Story of a Boy and a Seductress 25

Personal Truth 35

Shadows of Independence. 43

Submission in the Muddy Water 51

Gong and Cymbal 59

Top-Down Organization. 73

The Groaning 83

Confidently Ever After. 91

Further Reading. 95

A Gift

I have something for you, my daughter.

I've been keeping it safe for years now, waiting for you to grow up. Tonight, I realize that it is time. No longer are you the carefree, little, ponytailed toddler that I carried on my hip. Gone are the days when you and I spent countless hours together in imaginary castles. Your beautiful art projects have disappeared from the refrigerator. Your baby dolls have been sleeping for many years now. Only memories remain of our silly games and fantastical stories. The make-believe fairytales have faded back into the whispers of our past.

A parent's influence lasts for such a short time in a child's life. Before I knew it, you became old enough to make your own decisions and reap your own consequences in life. So my job was simple—to raise a young lady from the time she was a tiny, helpless baby. I taught you to brush your teeth and comb your hair. I forgave you and encouraged you to live boldly in faith. I taught you that you were safe and loved. I gave you the tools to succeed outside of your childhood home.

But tonight, I notice that you are stepping into the world and into a vast sea of stories about who you are and who you will be. These are no longer the tales that only live on the pages of your favorite books. These stories inspire the question of "who am I?" and will haunt your every decision. For any girl, identity is important. Along the way, you will eventually trust one of these many storylines. You might be lucky enough to hear the pure and simple truth, but more often than not, your ears will be overwhelmed with lies. Believing those lies can actually draw you away from who you are meant to be.

So I am giving you the gift of an ancient story. This is a story of character, a story of love and of sacrifice. It is a story of new hopes and amazing dreams. It has a happy ending that will certainly come true. When this story was passed to me, I was hypnotized by the beauty and simplicity of this ancient story. As you now venture off to become a woman, you will remember who you are and from where you came. You will meet an amazing guide and comforting friend. This story will become your story.

Our great story doesn't begin on the day of your birth. Nor does it begin with mine. No, this beautiful tale opens long ago, before anything was made.

It was still.

Empty.

Blackness all around.

There was nothing but a voice.

The voice spoke, and light appeared. The voice spoke, and water collected. The voice spoke, and living sprouts of green pushed through fresh earth. The voice created the earth, the stars, and life itself. This voice that ushered in the beginning of our story has a name: Wisdom.

Wisdom floated over the waters of the new earth. She hovered there waiting for her Master to speak again. She loved His gorgeous world. Bright, clear oceans sparkled, reflecting eager rays of the baby sun. Tiny, new leaves sprinkled every tree and the healthy moist soil. A robin's small sweet song overwhelmed the silence that was the beginning of our story.

Wisdom was here before any of us were born. Wisdom actually pieced together God's most intricate creation—mankind. She remembers the start of our journey, before we were. But even tonight, her voice still speaks to remind you of your story.

And so, my daughter, I pass this story to you. This is, at first glance, a guide to rights and wrongs, happy turns and sad endings. I hope it will teach you to distinguish between the wise and foolish paths in our world and help you find your beautiful feminine place in it. There are so many voices that will tell you which way to go, who to trust, and how to act. This story will be your lighthouse and touch point for decisions you will make as a woman. You will recognize, strive for, and actively be a beautiful female because of these wise words that were passed to me from our ancient sisters of the past.

You may not have recognized it until now, but Wisdom calls to you. She has been quietly repeating the same song since the beginning of the world. She sang to mothers, daughters, grandmothers, sisters, widows, and orphans from the first female breath. She knew you before you were born. She patiently follows you through every step on your path. And even now, she continues to speak to you.

Listen, my daughter, to this story preserved by those whom have gone before you. You may not yet have wondered where you fit in God's lovely creation. You may have unanswered questions and many unasked questions as well. This story is powerful enough to carry you through the rocky and dark questions that you have yet to even imagine. Or you may think you have everything figured out right now. You may reason that you have no need of advice: I am not in your place in life, I had a different background, and I could never fully understand yours. It is true that not one of us has yet encountered all the winding dilemmas of life. There are twists and turns we will never expect. But this story of Wisdom is life for all who hear it, no matter where we begin.

You need this story like you need air to live. Wisdom finds you wherever you are: single, seeking to be married, caught in a dangerous relationship, and even in beautiful patterns of love and service. Each woman on this earth has a place in God's creation, and He has carefully and wonderfully made you to live a beautiful life. The story I pass to you is from the lips of the Creator of all things. He made the ground on which you stand. He gave you the eyes to enjoy each passing sunrise. He formed the very air you breathe even now. And He speaks Wisdom into your heart and mind so that you will remember that you are His.

We have all been in different places when that voice of Wisdom speaks. Some of us were young and impressionable. We had not yet decided where our feet would land. She was able to guide and comfort us as we began the journey. Some of us were so far down a path that we could not even see where we began. She found us beat up and broken, tired of travelling at all. Some of us discovered her by surprise, as she jumped from the bushes at the most unexpected turn. She overwhelmed us and changed our course suddenly. Still for others, she held on to our arrogant hearts for some time. We knew she was there, but we did everything to ignore her persistent cry. But she was always there, no matter where we were.

So, daughter, listen to her call. Even as I teach it to you, her wise story daily guides me. There are none too old or knowledgeable that cannot love her words of correction and comfort. Each of us lives a lifetime in the living pages of this story, whether we realize it or not. Each of us is there with you, recalling the first few hard words Wisdom spoke to us. We were all lost and skeptical at the beginning. We were embarrassed and sorry for the things we had done. We were not quite ready to give up our own understandings. We were all afraid of our place in the great story.

Not many have spoken clearly about the gentle whisper of Wisdom to women, so I hope to speak those words a little louder so you too can hear. But even when the volume is turned up, it can still be unclear where this story really goes. There are points where this cosmic riddle is too hard to figure out. We have only caught a glimpse of the truthful story from time to time. We have even hated this ancient story when it departed from the storyline of our heartfelt desires. But now we will explore the teachings of Wisdom to understand her abnormal ways. We will unfold the stories and metaphors and puzzles of Wisdom—why she does what she does.

Be assured that in spite of the difficulties, this is an amazing journey to freedom. You will peek at the secrets of love. You will experience a heart of unending patience. You will begin to see yourself as more beautiful than precious diamonds. Your relationships will blossom into a strong bond of commitment. You will build off of a deep and unfathomable foundation that will never crumble. You will hear Wisdom's call, and you will be profoundly blessed.

But be warned, my daughter. This emotional tale is unlike the gossip you will encounter over coffee. You will not satisfy your proud heart or escape your unexamined ways with these chapters. Our story peels away your walls and expectations, and it even scandalizes the knowledge you may have gained from other foolish teachers. It will leave you wondering more than when you started. You will question who you are and where you are going. It will tear down your defenses and blatantly tell you the truth.

When you listen, don't be surprised that the foolish revolt against you. They will combat this ancient story with the modern knowledge of our world. There are doctors, psychologists, magazines, reality shows, movies, blog articles, books, specialists, and support groups that will offer alternative advice to keep you moving along their path. Don't be shocked when they discredit and laugh at the simple ancient identity you hear as your own. They will encourage you to take another path than that of Wisdom. They will entice you to follow their ashamed hearts. They will encourage you to join their silly schemes. But do not follow for if you do, you will risk forgetting the sweet voice of Wisdom who calls after you, even now.

Although the foolish blindly walk in a world of spurious visions and candy cane lies, that does not spoil the precious gift that has been given to us. I pray one day that they will be brave enough to see. But, my daughter, I know you are ready for your story.

Dust, Life, Death

Every great story begins outside of ourselves. It starts as a tale that captures our attention. We fall in love with the characters. And before we know it, we are caught up in a grand narrative built by the words of another. From the lips of a Story-Creator, Wisdom draws us in.

So lean in close, my daughter; listen to your story. It is an ancient story that comes from the very beginning of time. The Creator of everything made a beautiful earth. He crafted delightful and amazing animals to soar in His heavens and splash in His sea. He designed gentle and incredible beasts to fill His world. But as soon as God carefully formed a human being, we discover the God of the Universe is patient and loving with His creation. There are many accounts of the wonders and terrors of this God, but here in the beginning, we have a tale that personifies His passion for the people whom He created.

Just listen . . .

The air is fresh and calm. A young sun wraps the new earth in a blanket of perfect warmth. The whole creation seems to take a tranquil sigh. A man called Adam is surrounded by creatures in this breathtaking garden. It is a glorious day of naming beasts and birds for the man. The Lord had brought him every animal: furry, feathery, scaly, large, small, brave, and meek. The man has the honored job of naming all the creatures of God. Animals of every kind arrive, each one submitting to Adam as their caretaker. Earlier they poured out from every corner of the green field, but now each recedes into the background as the earth falls quiet again. Except for the slow trickle of the cool, clear stream, the sounds of the first birds and beasts fall hushed.

Even though the newborn world is filled with creatures, the Lord is concerned because His man is "alone." Even after Adam named all the wonderful creations, not one of them matches God's great masterpiece of man. I wonder what God is looking for? What kind of helper is necessary for this man? This human can carry out all his tasks easily. The perfect world in which he lives shelters and feeds him abundantly. He can take care of the Garden. He has dominion over God's animals and birds. The open, happy connection with God keeps him from any want or need. But yet God is concerned.

Adam's eyes become heavy. Velvety soft ferns cushion his head as a wave of relaxation rushes over him. Peacefully, he falls into a deep, perfectly sound slumber. There he lies sleeping, alone.

The Lord formed Adam limb by limb from the very dust where he now sleeps. He breathed on that dry form in order to fill this man with life. The man was gently placed in a stunning garden with life and water and plants surrounding him. But now, the Lord will create yet another creature in a very special way. The Lord gently pulls up the skin on one side of the slumbering Adam and takes his rib.

This creation did not come from the dust of the earth. This creation did not magically descend from heaven. But right out of the middle of God's fleshly image comes forth a new life. Adam's warm living bone is the foundation for a magnificent creature that could not yet be found on the earth. The Lord carefully and intentionally builds a helper who completely matches Adam. None of the animals were able to fulfill this role, this special companionship. This helper is unlike anything that had been formed from the dust; she is actually being sculpted from another creation: the man. But the man sleeps on, unaware of God's gift of new life, which is born from his very side.

As consciousness dreamily drifts back before the man's eyes, Adam catches a glimpse of an animal that he can't remember. She is incredibly attractive and yet so familiar. Wait, he thought, this is something entirely different. Blinking vigorously, so as not to lose sight of her, the sleepy haze melts into a magnificent vision. Adam slowly stands up from his grassy bed, gasping between the lumps of emotion welling up in his throat. She moves smoothly, in a flaw-less rhythm to the man's quickened heartbeat. Adam's tiny overjoyed tears blur the glorious procession as God presents to the man his long-awaited helper.

"Bone of my bones!" cries Adam. He recognizes this great deed of his Creator from the first glance. The Lord had constructed a being that was his impeccable compliment. "Flesh of my flesh," he whispers as she steps even closer. He embraces her soft warm cheek with the palm of his hand. His other arm cradles his own side, from where she was taken.

"I will call her woman, because she has been taken from man," Adam declares gazing into those familiar bright eyes. His task of naming God's creatures was as glorious as ever when he gives his bride and flesh-mate his own name. He confesses by her name that she is from him, with him, and at his side. There is something special and unique about this relationship. No other creature was yet created so intentionally from another. The very life that God gave Adam was the intrinsic foundation for this woman. The Lord found Adam to be incomplete; his loneliness was not good. Man was not created to roam the Garden to live independently. And now, neither was the woman created to be alone. They were created for flesh and bone unity, and God's creation is now good.

God's gifts are poured upon Adam and Eve as they were extraordinarily created in the image of God. They openly walk and talk with the Lord, and they completely do what they were created to do. Adam names and rules the creatures of the earth, and he is also given to be its gardener and protector. Eve is given the gift of bearing human life in her body and being a help to her husband. Their special tasks flow easily from the handcrafted bodies of their Creator. They were created to please God and to please one another. They exist together as one: a complete human. Both man and woman, naturally and joyfully, live in the gifts that they were given. God says this is certainly good.

Even more, God has a people who trust Him. They look to their Creator for answers; they respect His boundaries and commands. They believe His Word and praise Him for His amazing work. This is the fairytale God has always intended for His creatures. He is happy to provide for their every need. He is ready to live with them forever; no death or sickness would ever touch His beautiful people. All is good in the Garden of Eden.

Daughter, you might say this is the first boy meets girl romance. All great love stories and fairytales echo back to this simple and pure relationship in creation. Our imagination can now only dream of a lover who is perfectly and completely complementary. When we consider love and companionship, as our Creator made it, we are transported back to this beautiful Garden of Eden and this amazing beginning of our story.

But another creature of God's hand lives graciously in the Garden as well. The Serpent is wonderfully created within the story of the sun and moon, the trees, and the birds of the air. He is fed and protected. The Serpent is placed kindly under mankind's governance just as every other creature. The beasts of the field, the birds of the air, and every living thing came to Adam to be named by God's pinnacle of creation. But the Serpent becomes a deadly tool in the service of Satan. The Evil Foe will use this good creation of God to lead the man and woman into a broken relationship with their Almighty Creator. Satan enslaves this Serpent to introduce the most poisonous venom to mankind: doubt.

> [The Serpent] said to the woman, "Did God actually say, 'You shall not eat of any tree in the garden'?" (Genesis 3:1)

Did God really say . . . ? The Serpent focuses his attention on tearing down the Word of God so that the woman will doubt her Creator. He is not hastily pushing the woman to disobey God. He is not asking her to disown her God or run away from His blessings. Rather, the Serpent leads her to only question God's words. Her internal inquiries begin.

Listen closely, daughter. This story is not to scare you into obedience, nor is it to condemn your already-broken soul. It's important to realize how the crafty and cunning destruction of the Evil One enters our lovely romance. I remind you of this villain to awaken you to the present danger of the Devil. This miserable scoundrel still feeds us lies. His malicious task is to focus our eyes on another god besides the Maker of Heaven and Earth. Satan twists God's good creation and pulls us away from His gifts. Wisdom's words, God's blessings, and His promises are cast in a destructive light from the mouth of this Enemy.

> And the woman said to the serpent, "We may eat of the fruit of the trees in the garden, but God said, 'You shall not eat of the fruit

of the tree that is in the midst of the garden, neither shall you touch it, lest you die.'" (Genesis 3:2–3)

Hmmm . . . What did God really say? Don't eat of any tree? No, no, he just said not that one. I wonder why not that tree. I guess there is a chance we might die. The woman has already begun to doubt God. She can't quite remember how Adam taught her God's command. *"The Lord God commanded the man, saying, 'You may surely eat of every tree in the garden, but of the tree of the knowledge of good and evil you shall not eat, for in the day that you eat of it you shall surely die'"* (Genesis 2:16–17). God actually said that they will surely, really die if they eat of this tree in the midst of the Garden. But alone with the Serpent, the woman recites this decree slightly more "open mindedly" than God gave it. The punishment of death is not as emphatic here, in her words. A simple truth from God begins to appear meaningless. A Creator's command seems not as serious. The Serpent smirks. He picks up on her doubt immediately.

> But the serpent said to the woman, "You will not surely die. For God knows that when you eat of it your eyes will be opened, and you will be like God, knowing good and evil." (Genesis 3:4–5)

The Deceiver blatantly lies to the woman! He plainly negates God's command to Adam: you will surely die. The battle lines are clearly drawn. God said they would surely die. Satan says they would not surely die. Whom shall she believe and trust? By this time, though, the woman is already doubting and questioning the "good" gifts of her Creator. To soften this declaration of war, Satan then mixes in a little truth to encourage her rebellion. He entices her further to become like God, knowing good and evil. The prideful curiosity of the woman inches her closer and closer to that fruit.

> So when the woman saw that the tree was good for food, and that it was a delight to the eyes, and that the tree was to be desired to make one wise, she took of its fruit and ate, and she also gave some to her husband who was with her, and he ate. (Genesis 3:6)

It's good fruit! Why would God keep her from this good thing? It looks like it will make her happy. It seems that it makes her wise. She probably will be a better person if she tastes that fruit. Besides, the snake assured her that she will not die. So the next thing she knew, she is looking, she is desiring, she is eating, and she is sharing.

The vicious attack that Satan launched was successful. The line between good and evil is triumphantly shaded gray. In retrospect, we can recognize the distinction between God's Word and a word that doubts. We are on the edges of our seat yelling, "Stop girl! Don't listen to that sneaky snake! He is telling you a lie!" We know God's Word is life-giving. God spoke the Word and things were created. His Word now even creates faith. His Word is true and will do what it says. But the Serpent looks as if he has won the day by tricking the woman to hold on to a lie and not the sure Word of God.

Daughter, today we live among a people of unclean lips, in a world of doubt. Words surround us, not expecting God to act. The woman did not expect death for her actions. Likewise, we do not expect that our transgressions are so great that they deserve the attention of God.

You may even be encouraged by this wicked world to wonder why God would command such things. When His words are hard, we are often compelled to understand the mind of God and make sense of His judgment, especially when it is hidden from our understanding. Adam's wife searched for the logic in God's command not to eat. She questioned God's reasons for forbidding the good fruit. Her rational mind in the created world overthrew the simple, irrational words of God.

My girl, you are an expert at following your heart, aren't you? Our emotions guide us into the dark places of sin, where our yearnings rule. Words of desires that spill out of sinful hearts clash with the delight of our God. The woman looked into the wishes of her heart and trusted her own judgment above God's Word. The woman desired a prohibited wisdom and fruit. She was lost in the selfish focus on her own needs.

The poor girl trusted Satan, the Father of Lies. We too, can hear his evil voice more loudly than our Creator's voice, sometimes. Satan's goal is to pull us away from the call of our loving Shepherd and fill our hearts and minds with doubt. This Wicked Ruler of the earth screams in our ear with the congregation of unbelieving people to make God's children confused. These words are the deceptions of Satan, who whispers, "God is wrong." The woman was centered upon herself and Satan's lies—not the external Word of her loving God.

Because she did not believe and trust God, the tree in the midst of the Garden transforms from a beautiful expression of relationship and love into a symbol of death. She was created to love God. The tree was given to both man and woman so that they could worship their Creator. They both were created to trust His Word and not eat of this tree. The woman was created to love her Creator by clinging to His Word despite the Serpent's lies, despite the desires of her heart, and despite her good reasons. Tragically, she did not love as she ought. She did not listen to the words of her Creator. She listened to the words of Satan and of her own heart. The God who created her to love and worship now finds her less than what she was created to be. She is an unloving, selfish, independent creature. She is now dead.

We are plagued in our life with the consequences of this woman's sin. We also were created to love our God, but we do not trust the words of our Creator. We do not cling to His Word. We look to our desires and emotions to guide us down the "best" path. We worship the god of personal happiness in our broken lives. We have forgotten our story, just as the woman in the Garden did.

Now you may think, I could have done it better! If only I were there to live up to the law of the Creator! I would not have dared to even touch that awful fruit. My ears and eyes would have remained only on the God who created heaven and earth! You may be so bold to believe that day after day, hour after hour, you would be satisfied only with the gifts God gave to you. Never would you consider that curious feeling deep inside, which draws you closer just to smell the forbidden fruit. Not once would you sneak to the tree, when no one was looking, just for a tiny taste. Your heart would not even consider if God was telling you the truth. You would never even wonder if maybe He was keeping something amazing away from you.

Sadly, my daughter, you fail even now. You fail to see that the woman was likewise blinded by her own righteousness and importance. She had already taken the reigns from God as the Almighty. She doubted that His Word about this tree was truth. We, too, are captivated with our own feelings and desires, dethroning the Almighty Word of God. We also are taunted by this Evil Foe that seeks our destruction. We now taste the bitter flavor of the knowledge of good and evil. We shamefully share the consequence of death for her sin.

I often ponder the silent attack of the Evil One upon you and all daughters in the faith. His tactics are nasty, so much that modern women have grown accustomed to shuddering at our first feminine picture. The woman should have discussed her newfound fruit discovery with the man that shared her flesh. So where is the woman, today, who is honored for bringing all matters to her husband? Instead she is honored if she makes her own independent choices. The woman should have checked her own desires against the wishes of her God and her husband. So where is the honored woman who denies her personal passions and dreams for the sake of others? Instead we are summoned to rally with her any and every desire, and we do not dare to rebuke her emotion. The woman was counseled by a word from God that first she changed and then ignored. So where is the honored woman that ignores the call of the world and quietly submits? She is forgotten in the modern story of women we hear today. Consequently, we soften the blow of this sinful departure from God's good creation, and we also try to ignore the perilous consequences of death. Satan and sin have disfigured this creation so much that it is distasteful to us women. We have no reason to echo God when He says, "It is good!"

Woman was deceived. But she was not alone in the Garden. Her husband that shared her flesh also shared her taste of deadly knowledge. He took the fruit that now dulled her eyes. Because they were one, he shared in the sins, death, and pains that were his bride's. In fact, he made them his own. Both man and woman descended into a changed garden, a changed relationship, and a changed world.

Little daughter, I look around at this terrifying world that you are now slowly entering—death and war, deception and fear. There are so many things that you will find lurking in the shadows. I pray that Wisdom will keep you from harm and danger. I pray that you will endure until Christ returns. I pray that you would remember the brilliance of God's good creation in the Garden that He intended for you. Even though it is a distant memory, this is your great story.

Named

"It is very good," once said the Story-Creator. Yet just a few words into the story, man and woman traded paradise for a lie. Man and woman chose a future of death. Man and woman now hide from their self-made horror story in God's creation.

> Then the eyes of both were opened, and they knew that they were naked. And they sewed fig leaves together and made themselves loincloths. And they heard the sound of the Lord God walking in the garden in the cool of the day, and the man and his wife hid themselves from the presence of the Lord God among the trees of the garden. (Genesis 3:7–8)

Both Adam and his wife shudder in fear. They have both eaten the forbidden fruit now. The first bite was great, but the bitter aftertaste was unlike anything they ever had. Cowering deep in the bushes, they feel nauseated from embarrassment and shame. Something is terribly different and dreadfully wrong. Instead of running into the arms of their protective Creator, all they want to do is scamper away. Far, far away. Unexpectedly, this taste of knowledge and freedom has turned out to be very bad.

Man and woman in the Garden suddenly struggle with the same "freedom" that we trip over almost every day. We like to think they were free to choose the good gifts of God, and they were free to earn punishment and death that was passed on to the whole human race. The problem is this woman and man were never free. They were captive to the Word of God simply because He made them His "good" creatures. There is never a time when man and woman existed as a blank slate; free to choose the path they desired. They were created for a purpose. They were to love God. They were made to carry out a job. The man was the gardener and the woman was a helper. They were not free to decide what they would like to do. When the woman was bound to believe the Devil's word instead, she was not free from God's decree. God punished the man and woman according to His Word and will. But they were never free-range creatures. Both retained their identity as His creation, but now Satan fights in God's world to enslave His creatures in doubt. Our world and the Evil One would have us believe that we are free as well, but we are not. We are bound to our loving God by our creation, and yet torn away and enslaved to sin in the present fallen reality.

What the world calls freedom, for us women, is an attack on our dependence on the life-giving Word of the Creator. The world calls us to question the true Word of God even now. Does He even exist? If so, where do we hear His voice? Is His Word really the Bible? If it is, then how can stories about far away times and places mean anything for us? Why would a good and loving God appear to play favorites among men? Why did He choose to do things this way? It just doesn't make sense. You see how the enlightened logic of our day calls God to defend His answers. Did He really say . . . ?

What the world calls freedom is truly a call back to the tragic exchange with Satan. Craftily he wears us down to believe the lies of unbound freedom. Satan wants us to make our decisions based on emotion and circumstance, not on the gift of a Word given from outside of us. Satan crafts a vision of God that appears weak, broken, sexist, mean, out of touch, and stupid. By doing so, Satan urges us to be alone—what he might call "free." Whether we are "free" from a man or "free" from our God, the Liar would never admit it is he who seeks your service. Satan wants you to be loosed from the Creator's bondage so that he can bind you to himself in shameful death. He wants you to be less than what you were created to be.

What the world calls freedom is truly an intense focus on the god of "me." Banners fly that encourage the right to choose, for our own bodies, for our own selves. We belong to no one. We crave "me time," alone from every created gift of God. Our parents and friends tell us over and over, "I just want you to be happy." Every day we are being encouraged to be self-reliant and not dependent, and this is defined as freedom. We see what is good according to our own self-ish desires, and we take it.

> And they heard the sound of the Lord God walking in the garden in the cool of the day, and the man and his wife hid themselves from the presence of the Lord God among the trees of the garden. (Genesis 3:8)

He watches the unhappy couple, like a parent hiding in the shadows, and calls them out on their sin. There were now many other "gods" in the picture. Whether it was the Serpent, personal desire, freedom, or their own understanding, the Lord God was no longer first in their heart, soul, and mind. He created them to be His own. He created them to live in harmony with His Word. He created them in His image so that they might enjoy being the creature of a God who provided everything. God would not stand for this. God will not tolerate anything less than what these people were created to be—His.

> But the Lord God called to the man and said to him, "Where are you?" (Genesis 3:9)

God finds His people in the Garden broken, ashamed, and with nothing. But He does not just let the unhappy couple go. He actually searches for Adam and his wife. He discovers them shivering in the bushes.

> "Have you eaten of the tree of which I commanded you not to eat?" (Genesis 3:11)

The booming voice of God shakes the solid earth deep in the shadows. The law of God comes crashing down on the beloved creation. What was once created good has now turned sour because of the transgression of God's creatures. His Word of command now brings shame to the curious creatures. They know they have failed. They knew it the minute they heard their God walking in the Garden.

From there, the brave man digs his own grave deeper. "This woman!" Adam exclaims, "This woman that *You* gave me! She did this!" When God asks the woman about this terrible mistake, she also deflects blame. "The Serpent! He was the one who tricked me!"

accuses the woman. Both man and woman could not even live up to their obvious sin that hangs in the Garden. Adam blames God for his transgression, and then he turned on his helper. The creatures He created and His world have now been changed by a broken relationship between creatures and their God. This world that now had gained knowledge from the tree of good and evil, also had gained sin. He confronts the man, woman, and even the Serpent with a now different description of His creation that has fallen into judgment.

First God speaks to the Serpent.

> "Because you have done this, cursed are you above all livestock and above all beasts of the field; on your belly you shall go, and dust you shall eat all the days of your life. I will put enmity between you and the woman and between your offspring ad her offspring; he shall bruise your head, and you shall bruise his heel." (Genesis 3:14–15)

This was once a treasured creature under Adam's loving rule. The Serpent was created among livestock and the other beasts of the field. He was just as protected and loved as any other animal. But after the deception, the Serpent's body is thrust on the ground. He is shamefully cursed above all the other animals. After the deception, his nature is no longer to love and respect man, but to be hostile to Eve's children. The Serpent no longer resembles what God had created.

Next, He turns to His people.

> To the woman he said, "I will surely multiply your pain in childbearing; in pain you shall bring forth children. Your desire shall be for your husband, and he shall rule over you." (Genesis 3:16)

The woman was formed to mother children gracefully and effortlessly. Not a twinge of labor pain, not the slightest worry about her parenting technique, not even an anxious moment of concern for her babies. But after she doubted, pain and toil would plague her unique task. Woman was given the honor to help Adam where no other animal seemed fit. She was given life for the purpose of union with God's man. After her sin, strife enters the loving relationship between man and wife. Woman no longer rejoices in her gift as helper; in fact, she strives against it. At the same time, man would now rule over her to complicate the power struggle. Woman no longer resembles what God had created.

> And to Adam (God) said, "Because you have listened to the voice of your wife and have eaten of the tree of which I commanded you, 'You shall not eat of it,' cursed is the ground because of you; in pain you shall eat of it all the days of your life; thorns and thistles it shall bring forth for you; and you shall eat the plants of the field. By the sweat of your face you shall eat bread till you return to the ground, for out of it you were taken; for you are dust, and to dust you shall return." (Genesis 3:17–19)

Adam was given everything on earth. He was the highlight of creation. Before this awful event, every task was light, joyful, and fruitful. What a vivid picture of the one flesh: man and woman! Even though Adam knew of God's command, woman gave the fateful fruit to him, and he took a fatal taste. Whether he loved her more than God or expected the judgment to come upon both of them, he is ultimately responsible for this serious transgression. He listened to the voice of his wife instead of the voice of the Creator.

Adam's work becomes backbreakingly hard. The earth itself is affected on account of Adam; it would no longer produce the glorious fruits given in the Garden. His life was no longer easy, nor everlasting. After disobeying, he is destined to sweat for food only until he returns to the dust of death. Adam and the earth no longer resemble what God had created.

This broken relationship with our Creator is still our reality today. The death and punishment in this tragedy is one we all share. Look around; no one has escaped the consequences of sin in this world. No one escapes death. We are all punished like our first parents in this fallen, broken life. We are children born into sin. The fallen world, the man and woman's broken world, continues to be our reality. All have sinned and fall short of the glory of God. Creations that do not do God's will are condemned to die.

Their history is our history. Their world continues to be our world. Their God is our very same God. We live with the consequences of our first parents' sin. Our work is hard. Our relationships are stressed. Our childbirth is painful. We struggle just to live day to day only to labor into the dust of death. We even throw the good gifts of God back into His face.

But this tragic story, my love, took a beautiful turn when we weren't even watching. Even though they brought this twisted situation upon themselves, He didn't leave the wretched creatures to die. He found them cowering deep in the bushes. While both Adam and his wife were hiding in shame, Wisdom called to them from their loving Father.

> But the Lord God called to the man and said to him, "Where are you?" (Genesis 3:9)

He finds the woman and the man in the Garden and fought back for the identity of His people. They were not an abomination outside of His salvation and love. God proclaimed that this woman and man were created to be something special, beyond what any creature could destroy. There were consequences for the broken relationship, yes, but there is a resolution to this problem on the horizon. There will be a solution to the lacking love and terrible mistrust. There will be a permanent reconciliation between the Creator and His creations. God called to them and gave them a simple, life-changing promise.

> The Lord God said to the serpent . . . "He shall bruise your head, and you shall bruise his heel." (Genesis 3:15)

God spoke the first Gospel message to this desolate couple. There was good news given in the midst of their sin. God told the evil Serpent that man and woman would have a Child that would dash his head to pieces. Now the Lord was not simply speaking to a slimy beast gone bad. God revealed a much bigger reality in His now broken world. Satan will be defeated. Satan will be crushed. There will be no crafty snake in God's restored creation. Our terrible decisions cannot separate us from God and His gifts. Without the enemy Satan and the consequences of sin, we are left with the simple recollection of His Garden of gifts. Even in the depths of their disobedience, God loved His creatures so much that He gave them a glimpse of this victory. There is forgiveness, right from the beginning. God gave a word that He will reverse all that man and woman had done.

Although they didn't see the whole story yet, man and woman believed God's promise of life and restoration. They knew they had done wrong. They knew that they would leave the amazing Garden of blessings. They knew they would walk a life of sorrow. But their story now focused on a promise of a renewed future.

> "The man called his wife's name Eve, because she was the mother of all living." (Genesis 3:20)

She is called Eve. Eve means "life." Adam's first task was to name all the creatures. Up until this point, his lovely woman did not bear a name. She was woman, taken from the side of man, flesh of his flesh. But now with the promise of God in the face of their sin, Adam proclaims her true identity: she is the mother of all the living. She will be the mother of the first children on earth. She will be the mother of the Child that would bring all of them eternal life. "Eve" is a gracious confession of love and forgiveness from the promise of God, spoken on the lips of Adam. When Adam looks at this woman, he remembers their story. She brought an apple, knowledge, sin, disobedience, and death. Yet when this man names his wife, Adam speaks God's promise back to the both of them. He forgives Eve. He stands in the stead of God and proclaims they will be saved. He calls her mother of all the living. He breathes on her the identity of God's restored woman.

Man and woman, created together, are also made for this: God speaks His promises, and we speak them to each other. We tell each other the story of a restored life with a loving God. Even when sin gets in the way of this blessed conversation, as it did in the beginning story of man and woman, Wisdom found them. Wisdom speaks that promise again and again from the mouth of God.

> And the Lord God made for Adam and for his wife garments of skins and clothed them. (Genesis 3:21)

The air is cooler in the Garden, now. The sun descends behind a withering tree. As the newly dead leaves float silently back to the dust of the earth, the shadow of God passes over His Garden. Two snow-white lambs scream. And they lay silent and motionless before their Creator. He gently lifts up the lifeless skins and covers the naked shame of man and woman.

Daughter, God hides their sin with this first blood sacrifice. Foreshadowing the Hero to come, God kills, sheds blood, and his people are reconciled to Him here in the Garden. Later, in a similar foreshadowing, He would do the same with temple sacrifices. Like much of the Old Testament, this sweet chapter prepares us to see an even more complete sacrifice that covers the naked shame of the whole world.

> Then the Lord God said, "Behold, the man has become like one of us in knowing good and evil. Now, lest he reach out his hand and take also of the tree of life and eat, and live forever—" therefore the Lord God sent him out from the garden of Eden to work the ground from which he was taken. He drove out the man, and at the east of the Garden of Eden he placed the cherubim and a flaming sword that turned every way to guard the way to the tree of life. (Genesis 3:22–24)

So into the world they trudged. Adam looks ahead to sweat and hard work, just so they can eat. How easy it was back in the Garden where God's good gifts abounded! Eve will soon be overcome with pain for her children. It only begins at childbirth and her toil will continue through their lives. It would have been joyful bliss to conceive human life in the safety of God's Garden. For the first time ever, there is strife between the man and the woman. Anxiety, fear, fighting, and sorrow will all lead to death for our earth's first parents. What happened to the natural and complete union of this "one flesh"?

We have certainly lived too far away from the Garden of Eden. We can't begin to smell the sweet grass or feel the perfect sunshine on our face. But we do have a word from a God who has not left His proud, broken people alone. In the middle of their journey of fear and sadness, Adam and Eve hold tight to the promise of God. In hope, they watch every baby in anticipation of the "promised seed" who will overthrow death. They savor the rich blessings of God that leak through the distorted sin-filled world. They speak the words of hope, life, and forgiveness to each other and their family.

Our story begins with tragedy, sacrifice, and a promise of forgiveness. The woman who was created beautifully, at first did not listen to the Wisdom that called from the mouth of God. She did not believe that His gifts were good, just as they were given. But Wisdom followed her. Wisdom comforted the woman in the shadows. Wisdom moved from the mouth of God over the tongue of her husband. Wisdom whispered, "I forgive you," while Adam called out her name, "Eve."

The promise of life and forgiveness is who Eve is. The first woman and mother crafted by the fingers of God bears the name of life—restored to whom God intended her to be. Every daughter carries her name, her promise, and her identity.

You are a daughter of Eve. You were created by the Most High God. You walk outside of the Garden of Eden, bearing the pain and strife of the world but also bearing the promise of the Hero to come. You have been given hope in the One who will smash the head of the Serpent. You have been found by the Word of Wisdom, and you will again live as God intended His creations to live. This is your story, but only the beginning.

The Story of a Boy and a Seductress

Outside of the Garden of Eden, we look around and see the children of Adam and Eve everywhere. No longer are man and wife hedged in among the bountiful trees. We walk through every corner of the dusty world. We walk farther and farther from that fateful day of death and promise. We walk next to one another, barely remembering who God said we are.

The beauty and peace of the Garden is a distant memory, a fairytale buried under years of dirt. We have forgotten where to dig to recover the riches of Wisdom. We have never even seen the precious jewels of peace hidden deep within our story. The glory of God's creation hardened into a lost legend over the years.

But suddenly, along the path of forgetful history, life is breathed back into our story. Just when we least expect it, a wandering boy enters the dull and dreary story into which we have learned to settle. In our ordinary everyday world, I see the foreshadowed Child of the Garden, right before my eyes.

> For at the window of my house
>   I have looked out through my lattice,
> and I have seen among the simple,
>   I have perceived among the youths,
>   a young man lacking sense,
> passing along the street near her corner,
>   taking the road to her house
> in the twilight, in the evening,
>   at the time of night and darkness.

And behold, the woman meets him,
    dressed as a prostitute, wily of heart.
She is loud and wayward;
    her feet do not stay at home;
now in the street, now in the market,
    and at every corner she lies in wait.
She seizes him and kisses him,
    and with bold face she says to him,
"I had to offer sacrifices,
    and today I have paid my vows;
so now I have come out to meet you,
    to seek you eagerly, and I have found you.
I have spread my couch with coverings,
    colored linens from Egyptian linen;
I have perfumed my bed with myrrh,
    aloes, and cinnamon.
Come, let us take our fill of love till morning;
    let us delight ourselves with love.
For my husband is not at home;
    he has gone on a long journey;
he took a bag of money with him;
    at full moon he will come home."

With much seductive speech she persuades him;
    with her smooth talk she compels him.
All at once he follows her,
    as an ox goes to the slaughter,
or as a stag is caught fast
    till an arrow pierces its liver;
as a bird rushes into a snare;
    he does not know that it will cost him his life.

And now, O sons, listen to me,
    and be attentive to the words of my mouth.
Let not your heart turn aside to her ways;
    do not stray into her paths,
for many a victim has she laid low,
    and all her slain are a mighty throng.

Her house is the way to Sheol,
    going down to the chambers of death.

(Proverbs 7:6–27)

Daughter, listen closely. This is the part of the story that changes everything. Out of the corner of my eye, I can see that simple boy. An orange sky warms the deserted streets with the final glow of safe light. He strolls to the edge of the park, just outside my kitchen window. Not noticing anything out of the ordinary, my attention turns back to a half-witty storybook and my afternoon tea. But after a few sentences more, the peripheral course of his blue shirt turns. Instead of flowing right out my window view, his steps cut left and he doubles back. Strange, I thought. Where is he going? Captivated by bored speculation, I begin to watch the wandering traveler. Not many are out at this time in the afternoon, so his lonely wandering catches my curiosity. Behind the sheer white screen, I see him. Slowly and casually. He turns. He sits.

He doesn't seem like he is going anywhere in particular. He doesn't seem like he has any schedule to keep. He just walks along, turns around, and aimlessly wanders. His young eyes smile; his happy face is quite content. He is not the least concerned that the bright orange clouds quickly fade into a deeper shadow of purple.

Lights along the street pop on as evening descends. The little pins of light stand at attention in good order, guarding the perimeter of the quiet park grass—that is, until you reach the end of the street, where the corner sharply turns into the trees. A gray crooked street lamp slouches at that terrible corner of the street where evil dwells.

The young man continues his journey, wandering along the dark paths, kicking a stone here and there, leaning briefly, putting his hands in his pockets, spinning unpredictably to his new destination. As I watch, he moves closer and closer to that crooked streetlight. Not because he is curious, necessarily, nor because the light is blurry and softer, but simply because he has no other destination, as far as I could tell.

If I could yell to him, if he would hear me through the second story apartment window, across the street at the other end of the park, I would tell him to turn around. All the children knew to stay away from that dark and dangerous corner. It is the place from where the young and foolish do not return. But my voice is too far away. My counsel is too late to have been heard. He is walking right into the trap. I can only sit and watch from afar.

And then I see her.

She slips into the misty light at the corner of the street. Red stilettos kiss the pavement with her confident sexy stride. That silky black hair transforms the dull gray streetlight into sparkling stars, almost resembling a shiny crown. Tossing her head a bit to reveal her deeply plunging neckline, she takes a long heaving breath and calls out, "Over here, you."

He hears her. He sees her. He walks directly to her crooked corner.

She slides right up to this young one under the street light. Her voice is as smooth as oil. She says hello using every bit of her tongue to enunciate the greeting. Her lips pout and puff with nasty little words of seduction. She pulls him a little closer, brushing her breasts up his chest as she continues to hypnotize him with sensual words. Gently, her finger slides across his collar bone, down one arm, to his hip. She catches his belt and smacks her body tightly against his.

Pressing her soft warm mouth on his, her kiss tastes like a deep rich chocolate. She slithers her tongue across his teeth and deep into his mouth. Both hands claw feverishly at his back as her body trembles with an intense craving. She draws back, her eyes stare directly into his. She leans forward biting his lip, and she leads him inside like a dog on a leash.

To my horror, he follows her into that dark little house. This cunning adulteress lies in wait for fresh young boys while her husband is away. She catches the unsuspecting with her tight dress and terrible lies. Even though I can't see inside that house, I can only guess what she is doing. She is seducing him as she has no doubt done with all the other boys she has captured in the past. She is lying to him to satisfy her own twisted desires. Yet He walked through her front door like an ox to the slaughter, or like a bird right into a trap. When inside, she'll rip off his shirt. She'll tear at his pants with erotic rage. Thrusting him onto the bed, she will lock him in the shackles between her thighs. Whipped and scourged by the beating of her powerful hips, he will become part of her sexual fantasy.

The poor foolish boy! He should have known better. Once she had him in her sight, she bound him in her chains. Her power is that this crafty deceitful woman looks and sounds too good to be true. She says all the right things. She cleans up to look so enticing. She has dutifully "offered her sacrifices," suggesting a pious heart. What young man wouldn't be aroused by her sweet talk? What ordinary boy could resist the temptations of her lips?

If any boy enters her house, he will never come out alive. It happens every time without fail. After this wayward woman takes her fill from these young men, she fills them with the same poisonous life of shame she lives. By uniting with this unclean woman, a foolish boy exchanges Wisdom for a lie. In fellowship with this diseased woman, he takes on her every dirty sin. If he only knew beforehand what would inevitably happen when her angry husband came home. A young boy might be sleeping, exhausted from the night of activity. But this jealous husband wakes him up in a rage. Thundering, screaming, crashing all around him, such a foolish boy would be scared beyond belief. This husband knows exactly what happened during the night—an unfaithful youth slept with his adulterous wife. There is no escape; there are no excuses; wrath will be dealt out to each of them. The unashamed woman will certainly pay her penalty. The young boy will die, and he never even saw it coming.

Daughter, it is Wisdom that gives you eyes to really see this unfortunate story. The unholy Serpent from the Garden of Eden has left its stench on this dimly lit street corner. The Evil One's delicious lies are now on the lips of the seductress. Echoing the lies of the Serpent that originally conjured up doubt in Eve, the words of the adulteress beckon this silly boy far away from the well-lit path of Wisdom. We begin to recognize our sister from the Garden in that tight skirt, a horribly transformed creature born of disobedience.

Now the evil league of snake and temptress drag out the young fools to be slaughtered. The Evil One lies and seduces by his wicked slaves to fight the Almighty God. By Satan's command, they lead all down the path of distrust, dishonor, and death. Deep into darkness, Adam and Eve fell with every bite of disobedience to their Maker. Darker than the valley of death, our foolish youth is covered in Satan's black dirty filth in this prostitute's house.

The angry husband who will righteously judge the disloyal couple is the very same God who cast Adam and Eve out of the life-filled
Garden. He was furious with His creations because they had not done
what He created them to do. This vengeful God was ready to destroy
His unloving creations in the flood. God's people have been unfaithful
since the beginning. Instead of honor, they gave Him adultery. His
chosen nation in the Old Testament, Israel, was protected and loved by
the God of Abraham, Isaac, and Jacob. He was jealous for their faithfulness, as a husband would expect of his wife. Israel cheated on their
first love, their first God, their only true God. Israel wandered and
chose other gods to love and trust. God was deeply wounded. He saw
them as a prostitute nation, taking another husband than the one who
gave His promise to them. Mankind has been whoring out to idols
of all sorts: money, power, independence, and self-importance. They
have forgotten the God who created them and who first loved them.

Do you remember who this Lord is? He made the earth, the
sky, the air, and every animal. His hands formed dry land: mountains and valleys. He molded a man out of dust and breathed life into
his lungs. He placed each star in the sky, and He knows the unborn
babies before conception. He designed every different and obscure
species and bug. He waters the flowers on the desolate mountainside.
He is the amazing Creator of all things.

But as powerful as He is to begin life, He is just as powerful to
end it in a simple word. Winds and waves, droughts and floods submit to His Divine Command. He actually drowned most of His creation long ago. Beasts and birds and babies went screaming to their
watery deaths because of the angry wrath of this God. He shows His
power, and His people fear the Lord.

This Lord does not randomly create and destroy. He simply expects His creations to remain His. The most amazing thing
about this all-powerful God is that He loves. Remember, back in
the Garden, He finds His creations when they hide in shame; He
rescues His children when they break His good commands. This
God loves His creation so much that He will give His very own Son
as a sacrifice for them. Even when wayward people try to escape
His love, God accepts the death of His own perfect son as payment
for their terrible sins. He loves His people so very much, even when
they forget He is their Creator.

And you, my daughter, even though you may have forgotten your story, He will not let you go. But your path has not been straight. You have not remembered His promise of old to you. You have turned from the good creation that He has made you to be. You believe the lies of the world over the truth of your Creator. You have expected Him to bend to your will. You are shocked He demands that you be faithful. You can't believe He wants you to remain His creature.

You should fear your God. You have not followed His commands as you should. You have tried to break free from His control of your life. You should be terrified that He will sweep you away just as He did the unfaithful masses in ancient times. You should be scared for your eternal future—will you remain in paradise with the loving God, or will you be locked outside with the gnashing of teeth?

This fear of His awesome and all-knowing power is the very beginning of Wisdom. And Wisdom calls to you in our story. You have no excuse. He has created you and you have not lived up to His perfect creation. Together we are broken down to dust, having nothing of value to offer our God. We know our hearts are full of deception, excuses, apathy, and selfishness. Even when we think we are following the rules, God surprises us with a higher standard and a stricter goal. We discover we had misunderstood. He had always demanded more. Fear is the beginning of Wisdom because we no longer trust ourselves to save ourselves—we are exposed and afraid and actually dead in our sin.

I look out the window. There is no movement from the house across the street. I know what happened. The boy is dead. He was killed on the path of darkness. He was slaughtered by the angry husband at the end of the street.

My gaze becomes sleepy, out my kitchen window. Scared sympathetic tears dried three days ago, yet I couldn't look away from that hopeless house. How many more will it swallow? When will the next foolish boy wander along, only to struggle for his last breath? Who can stand up to that terrible, crafty, evil woman?

Early in the pale gray morning hour, I suddenly see a light flicker in the window at the crooked corner. A soft and clear white fire pierces the morning mist. A candle seems to be rekindled from the deadly quiet shadows. I can barely make out the figure of . . .

could it be? The boy? I am almost sure of it, squinting, moving closer to see. It is the likeness of that foolish youth who wandered into the Temptress's house. But there is a commanding pride now shining from this triumphant boy's face. He is not dead, after all? He is alive!

After three long days, the boy bursts from the treacherous tomb. He walks right out of the front door. The first yellow light of dawn shines on his satisfied smile. His clothes even seem to radiate with victory. I watch him fill his lungs with the sweet breath of a new day. By this time, the shabby little gray light at the end of the street is swallowed by the rays of the dawning sun. All the other streetlights bow to this bright and awesome morning. And the boy steps forward, down the right path.

My daughter, what I just witnessed was the incredible journey of a boy who smashed the curse of the Evil One. He walked into her house of death willingly. He knew how many she had slept with. He knew the evil in her heart. He knew her wickedness would kill him. But our Boy still walked inside. She delivered him to death because of her wandering adulteress heart. She tried to pull him away from the good and faithful path, but ultimately, she was not strong enough. He was no ordinary man. He knew no sin. He was the Son of the Most High God. He was the Word of God Himself.

This Temptress continued the legacy of sin from the Serpent from so very long ago. But this Boy is the One promised to Adam and Eve back in the Garden of Eden. We were told that the evil Serpent would bite His heel, but He would not die. No, this Boy would rise up and crush the head of this Evil One. Now He did and there is nothing more to fear! The Boy won! He never fell prey to her lies. He never lay in her diseased bed. Even though we saw Him walk into the dreadfully dark house of death, even though we watched Him fall dead, even though we cried and lamented as He took her foolish path, this Boy defeated the curse of death. The Evil One has been silenced, and the inheritance of the Temptress no longer has any power to destroy.

Of course, now you recognize your story. Jesus Christ walked among the footsteps of a simple people. Jesus stepped innocently into the house of the Evil One, not because He was tricked, but rather because He knew this was what must be done to save the foolish ones. He had to go all the way to death to satisfy the wrath of that Angry Husband; the one who demands payment for sins committed.

God never compromised His righteousness and justice. From the very beginning of creation, God declared death to those who disobeyed. Although Jesus never sinned, He embraced the rebellion of all people when He faced the Evil One.

But Jesus Christ did not stay dead. God raised Him up to eternal life. The Father was well pleased with His Son who did no wrong, who walked in the way of Wisdom, who would give His righteous crown to an undeserving, adulterous people. This, my daughter, is your story.

But something beyond wonder happens next. Just when we thought it was simply amazing that this young man comes back to life and turns back the curse of death, there is even another chapter to our story.

The Boy walks out of the silent tomb that quiet morning hour and seems to stall in the middle of the front yard of that terrible little house. Slowly, He turns back to gaze at the door from which He came. His right hand raises as if to point back to the passage through death. A smile bursts from His shining face. His eyes widen. And something rustles behind the dark threshold.

White lace flutters from the door frame. Under the gleaming streams of fabric emerges a slender soft foot. Delicate fingers lay hold of the rotten gray house. She glides halfway outside. A whisper of wind tosses a golden curl behind her creamy white shoulder. A magnificent woman returns this boy's loving smile. Stretching her toes, she dances toward His outstretched arm. He gently catches her, cradles her in an embrace, and effortlessly carries her away from that house.

The Evil Temptress was surely dead, but a new and beautiful creature stood in her place. The Boy brought forth a restored woman, a beautiful bride, a new life. When He walked away from His tomb, He did not go alone. He waited for His lovely wife to share eternal life.

And so it is with our story, my daughter. Jesus did not rise from the dead for himself. He paid the death toll so that His bride, His people, would follow Him out of the tomb. God's people are restored with the honored title of Bride. It was no accident that many of the parables Jesus told included a bridegroom and a wedding feast. The faithful people were very familiar with this relationship language with their God. So Jesus exchanged His pure heart for a black one stained by sin.

He exchanged our filthy rags for the splendor of righteousness. We are restored beauties by the blood of Christ. We are welcomed at the great wedding feast because Jesus dressed us in His garments. We are the holy people of God because Jesus washed us whiter than snow.

Jesus revealed that He was the Bridegroom for the people of God, and our hearts swelled with hope—He has finally come!

But the unfolding story of His joyous wedding, no one expected. No one ever saw that His blessed Bride would step out of the deadly, dark cave. No one would expect that such a sinner would be cleansed by His blood dripping off a cross. No one predicted that He could give such a gift of life to a girl.

Again, our God loves His once shameful and dirty creatures. In fear of our awesome and terrible God, we welcome a covering of righteousness from Jesus. Just like in the Garden, all sin and shame hides behind those snow-white clothes: Jesus's perfect life. Because of the gift of Christ, His death as a blood sacrifice, our Creator only sees His beautiful creation when He looks at us. We are wise because Jesus is the Wisdom that covers us.

And so, the Evil One has no power over you. The lies of the Serpent and the tricks of the Temptress are exposed. You see the deadly path. You watch your continual foolish choices beat up this underserving Son on the path. Now you recognize the horrible house where you act like an unfaithful woman. You cower behind an innocent Boy who stands between you and an Angry God. You cry as He is lifted up and slaughtered in your place. You fervently watch for His resurrection. It is joyful relief when He walks away from the tomb you led Him into and does it for you. Now you trust in the Boy who saved you from the Evil One and you know the outcome of your story. Wisdom lives. Evil perishes.

You, daughter, are Christ's beautiful Bride. But you walk in the wisdom of this story, not because you are so strong and crafty. You walk because He cleared the path. He moves your legs, one by one, in His footsteps. He took your shame and covered you in His white victory robe. You walk in the wisdom of this story on account of this Boy. From the Garden of Eden to the house on the corner, God has been looking forward to the day you stepped out of the curse of death into a new life. You have been restored to the beauty and wonder of God's creation. You are shining with the vitality of Christ. By no merit of your own, you are perfect. This is your story.

Personal Truth

Daughter, you are a special part of the epic salvation tale. This story from the outside speaks words of fresh hope, eternal beauty, and a faithful Savior into your ears. But here your personal story collides with the ancient forgotten tale. You are reborn a Bride, at the very same time you wander—lost in the twists and turns of your own individual short story. Given a new life, even today you are still trapped—confused in your private darkness, fearful and distracted from our one true hope. Trusting the precious story, we all still struggle to expect the happy ending we heard will come.

Our story is much harder than we would like to admit, sometimes. The twists and turns we experience can break our heart and shift our focus. The choose-your-own-adventure reality can take us down a road we never saw coming. The bright path we expect to see is hidden in this dusty, dirty world. The relationship between man and woman doesn't seem to go as smoothly as it did in our story of creation. Our created identity has been buried under layers of sin. I, myself, have wondered over and over, "Who am I supposed to be? What am I supposed to want? Where is the place for a girl like me?"

For you and for my own wandering ears, hear the call of Wisdom. She quietly sings this story to all the children of the promise. She whispers our ancient story right into the middle of our loud and hectic lives. She has followed you through every dark valley, even when our paths have led us far away. So listen, my daughter, to our wise, dear friend; can you hear her voice?

> Blessed is the one who finds wisdom, and the one who gets understanding, for the gain from her is better than gain from silver and her

profit better than gold. She is more precious than jewels, and nothing you desire can compare with her. Long life is in her right hand; in her left hand are riches and honor. Her ways are ways of pleasantness, and all her paths are peace. She is a tree of life to those who lay hold of her; those who hold her fast are called blessed. The Lord by wisdom founded the earth; by understanding he established the heavens; by his knowledge the deeps broke open, and the clouds drop down the dew. (Proverbs 3:13–20)

Blessed are you, my daughter. You found her. You've discovered that you have been captured by the Word of life. Wisdom did not forget God's great promise to Eve at the very beginning of our story, nor does she forget you right now. You have been dressed in the riches and honor and life by the Word of Wisdom. You are now the Bride that walks, the light that lives, the wise woman who feasts at the Tree of Eternal Life.

Wisdom was there from the very beginning, and she finds you even now. As she hovered over the waters in creation, she now hovers over you in this story. Wisdom saw the goodness of God's creation before we even existed. She was there acting out every creative word God could utter. She says,

The Lord possessed me at the beginning of his work, the first of his acts of old. Ages ago I was set up, at the first, before the beginning of the earth. When there were no depths I was brought forth, when there were no springs abounding with water. Before the mountains had been shaped, before the hills, I was brought forth, before he had made the earth with its fields, or the first of the dust of the world. When he established the heavens, I was there; when he drew a circle on the face of the deep, when he made firm the skies above, when he established the fountains of the deep, when he assigned to the sea its limit, so that the waters might not transgress his command, when he marked out the foundations of the earth, then I was beside him, like a master workman, and I was daily his delight, rejoicing before him always, rejoicing in his inhabited world and delighting in the children of man. (Proverbs 8:22–31)

We can trust her word. She has a deep knowledge of the ancient story before the things ever took a turn for the worst. She can recall the beauty and goodness that God's creation intended to be. Wisdom whispers our true story from the hidden beginning into our present darkness.

> In the beginning was the Word, and the Word was with God, and the Word was God. He was in the beginning with God. All things were made through him, and without him was not anything made that was made. In him was life, and the life was the light of men. The light shines in the darkness, and the darkness has not overcome it. (John 1:1–5)

Wisdom moves through our story as a word of life, and not just the first breath of life, but she now continues to tell the story with the breath of a new life. Wisdom was in the beginning; Wisdom was in the life of the Boy. Wisdom was the light that entered the dark house on the corner. Wisdom shines in the darkness from within the beautiful new bride.

> The true light, which gives light to everyone, was coming into the world. He was in the world, and the world was made through him, yet the world did not know him. He came to his own, and his own people did not receive him. But to all who did receive him, who believed in his name, he gave the right to become children of God, who were born, not of blood nor of the will of the flesh nor of the will of man, but of God. And the Word became flesh and dwelt among us, and we have seen his glory, glory as of the only Son from the Father, full of grace and truth. (John 1:9–14)

Christ is the Wisdom from the beginning of the world. Christ is the Wisdom that became flesh and dwelt among us. Christ is the promise that defeated the Evil One in the darkness. Christ is Wisdom for you.

Christ is Wisdom who calls you forth as the beautiful Bride. The voice of Wisdom, the Word made flesh, makes this your story. Without spot or blemish, you can walk through this dark world of shadows. With the ears of Wisdom, you can endure the lies of the Evil One. With the eyes of Wisdom, you can see your story clearly once again, beginning to end.

Yet you did nothing. The most amazing and confusing part of our story is that Wisdom has played all the parts. It was never your choice to be wise. It was never your desire to die. It was not even one step you took to be closer to Wisdom. She came in from the outside and changed your life. And she has never stopped calling to you.

Looking back over my own individual story, there were too many opportunities to see the struggle between men and women and the distance between a people and their God. As a child, I grew up listening to adults praise "gender-neutral language" and bash traditional roles—barefoot and in the kitchen stuff. I was taught that girls could grow up to do anything and be wary of the men who said differently. I watched funny television shows with Mom rolling her eyes at Dad, again. Even as a little girl, I sensed that there was something troublesome going on here.

Then one day, it was my very own heart that was torn. I trusted a young man to love me. But the ups and downs with him left me dizzy. After we endured several months of painful relationship toil, he moved on to another girl. We both said things we regretted. We both ended up wounded. The ancient strife between God's creatures had affected my own life. The pain of this failed love turned my hopes sour.

My experience in this world has taught me a much different story than Wisdom tells. My broken heart is still tender and teaches me to be less trusting next time. Every disappointing relationship leads us to guard our emotions, not expect too much, and certainly not let ourselves dream about a happy ending. Experience wants us to remember our own joys and the pains and learn from them. Experience screams out from inside our heads and our hearts. Experience presumes we can become an expert in our fate.

While we honor the experience, this is not the only way we learn about the truth of our story. Looking back to the beginning, the first people, Adam and Eve, shared the perfect relationship, handcrafted by God himself. But there, the temptation of experience attacked God's couple. Eve was certainly tricked by the sneaky words of Satan in the Garden. She listened to his awfully seductive words, and then she desired the forbidden fruit. In culmination, she trusted her own judgment and took "knowledge of good and evil" when she bit into that fruit. Experience was born, and both the man and the woman won death.

Experience trusts the god of "me." Internal feelings and personal decisions guide us in the realm of our experiences. But Wisdom tells of a truth that lies outside of our emotions. Wisdom tells a story even beyond our comprehension. Where experiences vary and change according to person and time, Wisdom remains the same from the very first word of creation.

Your story today is tangled with experience, but Wisdom holds you steady in an eternal truth. Your story of late is painful and dark, but Wisdom carries you into the light. Your story right now looks like a disobedient Eve and a wayward adulteress, but right now Wisdom calls you Christ's confident Bride.

Even God's people, Israel, were led away from this loving story time after time. It was only a short experience in the desert before the Israelites wanted to go back to captivity in Egypt. Moses was only on the mountain of God for a little while before the people created an idol from gold to worship. Experience in this world quickly eats at our heart of faith. It chips away the Wisdom that we hear is true.

From the bloodline of God's chosen people, Jesus entered into the world of experience. He wept. He became angry. He even prayed before His death asking if there was another way. The pain inflicted by a sinful people in a messed-up world can even break the Son of God. He hurt, He cried, He died—all in our realm of experience.

Jesus, however, knew of another truth beyond experience. He focused on the promises of His Father. This God said He would never forsake you. He said you were loved and honored to sit next to Him on the throne. God said there is a beautiful land created just for you, with none of these terrible experiences. Jesus trusted these promises over His deadly experience on our earth.

We know this story is true because Jesus rose from the dead, just as He promised He would. Life eternal is His. He proved that the promises are true. And so we learn the deceiving truth about our own experiences—they are not as real as His promises. When God tells His people that they will inherit the earth and there will be no more tears, God is talking about forever. Our miniscule experiences will not endure. They are truly not as defining as they often feel.

But our experiences have made us very cautious, especially when we are considering our identity. Because you were teased about being too girly, because you were hurt by that jerk, because you were abandoned by your dad, you have learned to shield yourself from that naïve trust in a Word from outside of our self-protected heart.

Because we have had some devastating experiences, we have taught ourselves to not trust God's bold promises.

My own experience also led me around in circles, yet it was not a harsh one that bruised my trust. I grew up going to Sunday school, having been baptized as a baby. My parents took me to church almost every Sunday. I could sing the hymns and recite the prayers. God's Word was always a part of who I was. But one day when I was older, I found "truth" feigning a thousand different faces. I didn't expect the things eternal I learned from the Bible would clash so violently with everyday life in the world. As I grew into a woman, I found myself questioning everything about this true faith as I baby-stepped into my personal grown-up experience.

Awakening as a teenager, I one day saw the face of the pastor who comforted me week after week during the turbulent path of middle school. She had a compassionate twinkle in her brown eyes and soft voice. I remember her mothering hugs and the beautiful ways she painted pictures with her words. My pastor, called and ordained by a traditional-style church, was a woman. For a simple teenage girl who went to church, this loving example of a woman was an encouraging experience. She inspired me to learn. She inspired me to grow. But there was a fuzzy darkness that hung about our heads.

I learned more about the Word of God. I grew to love the revelation given to me, outside of my own turbulent teenage heart. I trusted in the hope of an eternal life and new earth. But ironically, the more this pastor told me the story, the more I began to hear the shame. The more I asked her about the truth, the more obscure the answers became.

I experienced an amazing woman who could love and speak about Christ and His church. But she personally had to change the story—the truth—that God gave to all of us by His Word. The changes began subtly enough: observing our own God-given gifts of service, then organizing the way we interpreted the creation of man and woman in Genesis 1–2. Consulting our own cultural climate concerning women, then making assumptions about the story that St. Paul tells in the New Testament. Our personal experiences, good or bad, began to construct the truth that we would confess as women in the Faith.

I did know that a truth must be somewhere. But it couldn't exist only in my head nor in my own short experiences; I certainly wasn't an expert on the truth of all things. The world was very disappointing and shallow when it offered answers. Hostile to the Word of God, advice from magazines, television shows, billboards, *et cetera* didn't have enough of a story to say anything of importance. Popular contemporary wisdom blew in every direction as quickly as the wind changed. Good friends seemed just as lost as I was; we were all figuring it out as we went along. As much as I wanted to believe in the equality of women, even in church, I understood that my experience was so small compared to the wonder of God. I must be missing something here. Everybody else seemed to be content to explain away these little sections of the Bible, so maybe I was just being too uptight. By the time I went off to college, I became extremely comfortable with ignoring large portions of God's Word. Of course, I had rational excuses for looking the other way.

By then, the world and evil lies had tainted my desire to hear the truth of scripture. My sinful craving for independence pulled me away from hearing God's external Word of discipline and love. The Devil twisted God's once beautiful creation in His eternal Word and left me with only a shadow of freedom to chase. My own experiences began to retell the ancient story of woman.

My daughters, beware of your own short story. The steps of your life will lead you to many places. Your ears will search for the answer. As I mentioned before, there will be too many places that will offer you advice. Your personal experience makes the vain world around you seem more real and true than the reality that is unseen. The work of your hands may feel more important than a work that was done for you. You might forget the hidden places where God's promises meet you—in water, a meal of forgiveness, a spoken Word of comfort—and you might chase after a meager happy life. Our experiences can lead us to deception if we give them primary importance. I almost forgot who I was. There was a time when I couldn't remember to whom I belonged. My experience left me alone to search for meaning and a place in this world.

Daughter, it is good to question the whys and hows of our faith when it drives us deeper into God's Word for the answers. He wrote this story long before you were ever born. He is the one that created the questions before you ever asked. He will be the one to give you

His peace and comfort, no matter what the answer turns out to be. It might be easier to ask our world to give us the answers we desire. It's certainly a temptation to look inside our own hearts to find the way. But Wisdom promises to sustain you with precious and true life-giving words, outside of your own heart and mind, and make your feet walk on straight paths.

Even though our experiences up until now may have been different, my journey becomes yours as well. Our story—beginning with the Word of God and ending with the Promise of life—is very much the same. Our story is not just about where we have been or where we are going. Our story is not the sum of our experiences. Our story is the truth about who we are. Most importantly, it did not begin with us. Our story reaches back to the story of Eve and a promise of a Boy to come. Our story follows the Boy into the house of shame and death where He dies. Our story walks confidently out of the house clothed in white into the loving arms of our Risen Hero. Our story continues this bridal march in the arms of our Savior as we weather our experiences. We are not defined by the individual stories of our present. We live as restored creations of the Most High God, chosen by the Bridegroom to walk forever with Him. That is our story.

Shadows of Independence

Not everyone wants you to hear this story. The "wisdom" of our world distracts us from the eternal answers that Wisdom whispers in our ears. We live in a place and time where her ancient story is hushed and ridiculed. The characters have been hidden; the vocabulary has been censored. The world attacks this story by shaming and confusing women. Our culture mangles and misunderstands our promised story that steadily breathes life behind the curtain of pain.

So many believe that we have already moved past the stinging issue of a woman's place in society, the home, and even the church. We, in America, now have such a transcendent and loving understanding of the equality of gender, nation, and race that the discussion is over. Even my own beloved church body seems to have moved past the conversation; we now only refer to the lines that were drawn between allowing woman's participation in a church voter's meeting and forbidding her voice in pastoral ministry. Still other church bodies encourage a woman into every position of authority, unashamedly as if there were never a debate. But in the midst of our story, watching you struggle, daughter, with your own identity, I remember again that this conversation is still white hot.

When I began my intense love and study of theology in high school, one particular question drove me deeper and deeper: "Who am I?" Yes, I know that is not the most important question in the realm of theology, with Christological heresies and all. But looking around in this world of men's voices, I had yet to experience the theological perspective of a female. Passionate, compelling, sound teachings have been faithfully spoken on the lips of gentlemen. A war of words about what "she" should do and not do have been shot back and forth. Caught in the crossfire, my expression of this ancient story always came full circle—how do I, as a woman, make this confession?

Quiet, late nights in the college dorm became my favorite time of retreat. Stale coffee kept me company while I read books and pamphlets and papers and anything that could silence the rerun of thoughts through my brain. The fluorescent multipurpose room gave light to my first readings of Genesis in Hebrew. I still remember fondly the cold metal table that supported my endless note scribblings. It was here that I only began to piece together this dusty story of old.

Studying the words in the Bible, I realized the teachings are shocking, but painfully clear. There are well-defined purposes for each gender. From the beginning man was created to work the Garden and name the animals. Woman was created with a womb to bear children. There are distinct differences between man and woman. "The head of every man is Christ, and the head of the woman is man, and the head of Christ is God." There are encouraged and forbidden things. "I do not permit a woman to teach or to assume authority over a man; she must be quiet." But in all of this there is an extreme disconnect from my "liberated" experience as a woman—and the Word of God.

Here I was, living on my own. I drove a car. I made my own decisions where to go to church and what to have for dinner. I was receiving an awesome college education with the expectation of entering the workforce. During these years of study and preparation, I stumbled into a love of ancient languages and had conversations with great minds of the present time. My liberated life made me wonder if I was really acting like a woman of God from the Bible.

Then in the middle of my junior year, a sexy, bearded man confessed his love for me and I was terrified! Wasn't my independent status, as a young college student, good? What would happen to "freedom" if I was joined to him? I was confident enough to continue following the headship of Christ Himself. But joined to another, the headship of this physical person would stand between me and the flow of His gifts. I wasn't so sure about that.

Almost a year later in our wedding sermon, the pastor warned us of this very fear, the weighty reality of joining two sinners together as man and wife. Marriage meant a word of correction, comfort, and forgiveness would be spoken to me by this man who stood before me. Marriage meant sickness and health, rich and poor, loving and supporting this sinner would be a part of what I woke up to every day. I would become one flesh with this guy—no longer fitting my image of being independent and free.

But then again, who told us we were ever free? The women's liberation movement, while trying to solve a perceived injustice, in the end inflicted serious damage on women. However, it was not simply a restructuring of our everyday choices about what is socially acceptable and what is not that hurt us. The damage is much deeper and profound. This liberated generation of women explored an ancient lie of freedom; women should be able to do whatever they want. They have fallen into a deadly story about a free individual able to make her own choices with her own body and her own life. And it has passed it on to you, daughter.

There is a grave problem with this redefined identity; it is not spoken from God. According to our Lord and His gracious creation of man and woman, neither were created to be unbound individuals. "The Lord God said, 'It is not good for the man to be alone. I will make a helper suitable for him.'" From the earliest beginning, man and woman were created for each other. Sadly, the cries of liberation have disintegrated into a pursuit of "alone-ness." We are told to become self-sufficient and to rely on no one. We mindlessly encourage each other to break the chains of dependence in the name of self-interest. Echoing from Adam's lonely walk in the Garden, this is not good.

Can you hear this old saga of lies that captured the heart of Eve? "Choose for yourself, girl," Satan whispers. Take knowledge and independence, it will make you more like God. But the Devil never said out loud that he trapped her in his evil service. He never told Eve that she would step out of the Garden, marked as a prostitute. He never showed Eve the life of filth that condemned her in a dark house of death. And the Evil One still plays these tricks with his tale of deception.

Daughter, we walk this unfaithful path, and we might not even be aware. We want to be independent, even from God. Satan has been lying and tempting the daughters of Eve ever since he gained a foothold. The Devil plays on our curious desire for enlightenment, especially when it draws us away from trusting the Word of God. The Evil One fuels our loud and hasty protests, and he laughs in victory when we invite other gods into our bed. Beyond the Garden, we stumble along in the darkness of this sinful world. We are fooled by sinful temptations of individuality and selfishness. We choose the wrong almost every time. We want to continue to live in our blind oblivious mess. But Jesus doesn't leave us here.

In our story, Christ exchanges His faithfulness and victory for your disobedience. No matter where you came from. No matter who you are. No matter what you did. Not just for lifelong Christians. Not just for those who have only just heard the call of forgiveness. He puts on you His robe of righteousness. Not just those in high standing, but the lowly too. Not only men and not only women. He clothes us all with His pure righteousness. We are alive only because of the Boy. Without sin, He walked our unfaithful path. He defeated the Evil One because we could not. He rose up in victory. And now His story becomes ours.

> For in Christ Jesus you are all sons of God, through faith. For as many of you as were baptized into Christ have put on Christ. There is neither Jew nor Greek, there is neither slave nor free, there is no male and female, for you are all one in Christ Jesus. (Galatians 3:26–28)

This describes our true freedom. Free to do what, you ask? That is a beautiful question. You are now free to be the creation of God. You are no longer trapped by the lies of Satan in a foolish world. You no longer are chained with worry about the deep scary sins in your heart. You are one flesh with Christ; you are free in Christ.

Freedom in Christ releases you from guilt. Freedom in Christ promises life, no matter what you do. Freedom in Christ can't ever be repaid. Freedom in Christ binds you close to your God. But this Christian freedom talk is perhaps tainted by our cultural understandings more than we would like to admit. When we say we are seeking freedom in America, oftentimes, we are really seeking autonomy. This is not God's gift to us. He did not create His creatures to be alone or autonomous. Remember in the Garden, it was not good that man was alone. A person who is influenced by nothing, beholden to nothing, connected to nothing, restored to nothing, is nothing to

God. A "freedom" from God and from each other is not what Christ delivers.

Rather, my daughter, our story begins with submission. Yes, it is a dirty little word in our culture today, but that was not always the case. God created His people, His whole creation in fact, to love and trust Him. He created all of it to submit to His Word. Imagine this relationship of submission through God's perfect eyes. He will give His people everything, fill their every need, protect them, and love them. Because they are His creatures, His people would trust His Word, cherish His beautiful creation, and live as His people—in submission. This lovely relationship was established before any sin entered the world. God was the head and gifted His creation to submit.

The Garden of Eden proved to be the first battlefield between God and His created-to-be-submissive people. Instead of trust, Eve doubted. Instead of love, she looked to another. Instead of submitting to her loving God, she ignored God's good creation and handed Him a broken relationship. But sadly, the attack on God's order of headship and submission did not stop there. The simple communication between Adam and Eve was disturbed by a selfish reordering of creation. Instead of man acting and speaking as the head of his family as he was created to be, his wife became the shameful spokesperson for the first couple. Where he should have stood strong and rebuked the snake for his lies, she appeared to make the decisions of eternity for the both of them. Their one-flesh partnership turned deadly now as they shared disobedience. No matter who took and ate the fruit, Adam is held responsible for the faith, speech, and action of his own flesh; himself; and his wife. Whether he acted out the sin or not, God charges him with the fall of humankind. Woman no longer helps, man no longer protects. God's good order quickly crumbled in the twisted game of sin.

As people increased on the earth, there was clearly something wrong. They did not submit to their God, so much so that there was more evil than there was good. God was so very angry about the terrible state of His creatures that He wiped out the entire earth in a great flood. Man, woman, and child died, except for a family of eight whom God chose. Noah was chosen to remember the loving relationship between God and His people. He submitted to God's call, even if it looked a little crazy to build that giant ark.

The story continued, and God fought for His beloved people. He chose Israel to be a great nation, a beautiful bride. He led them out of slavery, He provided food and water for them in a desert wasteland, He protected and loved His creatures. Israel continually forgot what it meant to love her God. Instead of trust, she tested God to perform. Instead of love, she took other gods. Instead of submitting to her loving God, she threw His gifts back in His face again and again.

Strangely enough, when God descended on the earth one quiet night as a baby, we were all awaiting a God to submit to. We looked for a great and powerful king that had the leadership to overthrow the strong. We looked for the impressive prophet who could cast out demons and heal the sick. We looked for a leader to guide us through our dark and shameful world. Little did we know that Jesus Christ was the one who came to submit.

We watched Him take comfort in the arms of a dirty teenage girl, wallowing in an animal's trough. We saw Him walk with sinners and prostitutes and eat with tax collectors and wash filthy feet. We heard Him say nothing when accused by the authorities on His way to judgment. We winced when He allowed himself to be beaten and mocked. We cried when He gave up His life by a torturous death on a cross. Christ submitted completely to this evil generation and to the will of God.

Our story tells of a lowly Boy that submitted to death. His submission is for you. He quietly knew that you should have been the one to endure God's punishment for believing the lies of the Evil One. He silently stepped into your path of destruction and submitted to punishment for you.

This gift of Christ's perfect submission now flows into our lives and our relationships. He reversed the unloving autonomy of Eve. He rewrote the ending to the penalty of death. He restored the wayward adulteress to eternal honor. Our story tells us that everywhere we don't submit in our sin-struck world, our confidence lies in Him who did. He has done it. He has submitted, and it is done.

But here we are. Some of us are torn by friends who scream autonomous freedom, but truly seek to gather support for their own life choices. Some of us are pulled by mentors who preach submission that entails acting in a particularly prescribed way. Every side of the passionate spectrum binds our conscience to do it the right way, to be a "real" woman. Our personal experience shows us we can be hurt by depending on another. Worse than that, for a Christian woman, God's Word speaks of a relationship that most of us have never seen. This biblical truth about headship and submission is not displayed, understood, nor desired.

Daughter, I am here to remind you of the forgotten gift God gives to women. He daily cares for you, protects you, forgives you, and loves you through one who is your head.

This story is our honored place in creation, in our faith, and in our home. I am bound to another, and He is bound to me. This amazing story is told as Christ stoops down before His Bride to wash her feet. It is told when He steps into a baptism of repentance for her sin. It is told when He extends His arms and dies so that she can live. He submits His honor, His life, His individuality to be united to the church. In turn, she lovingly trusts Him as her head.

The proper understanding of our freedom is in a story where we are bound to another.

So where our lives meet in relationships—relationship between God and man, between head of church and submissive hearer, between husband and wife, between parent and child—we meet in Christ. Our relationships are made right because Christ stepped in and submitted to the Word of His Father for Eve. He substituted His own submission for all of Israel. He carried the burden of the disobedient child and restored Him to a loving Father. He submitted to death, even death on the cross, to cover the shame of His cleansed Bride. He submitted so that you, daughter, are set free from death and sin to be God's creation once again.

And so it's not really a question of what to do now. You will just do what God created you to do from the very beginning. No checklist or report card. You are free again to live in a good relationship with your Creator. It doesn't depend on you and your choices. Wisdom gives you restored freedom. But right in the middle of our story, you will find that you love what He loves. You will notice that His good is your good. You will find a community of men and women, slaves and free, Jews and Greeks that believe in His work alone. You will recognize what a blessing it is to be His beloved creation, and you will desire it more and more.

Bound to Christ, you are free to submit once again. So our story continues today, remembering who we are. It's not always as easy as some would have you believe. You might be wondering what to do now. You are probably ashamed because you haven't done it right. But you are free from your choices on account of Christ. We are truly free from evil, death, and fear in the loving arms of our Bridegroom, Christ. When the world fights to have you forget, Wisdom remembers your story: you are one flesh with the beloved, righteous, resurrected Son of God.

You are free to be God's woman.

Submission in the Muddy Water

Daughter, Wisdom speaks plainly to you right now. To call a thing what it really is—not to lie or deceive ourselves anymore about this story—we now must make some bold confessions. Remember, I told you this would not be easy. The hidden realities that we are about to admit together will forever change you. Here we fight to hear the truth and purity of God's Word alongside the words of love and faithfulness given to His beloved creatures.

A brief inhalation in the fresh sunshine reminds us of the wonderful gifts given in the Garden. Everything was new and unblemished. It's no surprise God created His creatures to love and listen. He was the head, His creatures submitted. God provided everything for His man and woman. Food, companionship, rest, life, and love. The people had an identity—submissive love.

Then across a dusty desert, the chosen people Israel had a long history experiencing God's love. He selected the small and insignificant people in order to make them great. God supplied everything for His nation—food in the wilderness, water in the desert, leadership through seas and darkness, salvation from oppression. He asked only one thing in return, "You shall have no other gods." It was good for His people to love and submit to their God.

Much later, a tiny baby, who was the Light of the world, cried out in the middle of a poor town. He was born in a manger, in the lowest position of submission to the Great and Almighty Father. This frail, stinky Child would grow to do everything that His head asked of Him. He taught the Father's Word, He remained faithful, helpful, and in submission. Even when Jesus prayed that His road of submission was too hard, He still continued down the path in silence. Jesus perfectly loved and submitted to God.

In our story, here, we watched our Hero stroll down a dark forbidden street. He walked through the door of certain death. He entered the threshold because of submissive love. He lowered himself to His knees to bathe the feet of His Bride, the church.

Submit to one another out of reverence for Christ. (Ephesians 5:21)

Suddenly we see the love that flows from one submission to another. If Christ loves His church, if Jesus loves His Father, if Israel loves her God, and if creatures love their Creator by submission, then it is a good and beautiful gift given by God. And we can be daring enough to love one another by the gracious gift of submission.

Paul begins this conversation in Ephesians 5 by exhorting the Ephesians to "be imitators of God, as beloved children." They are growing up into Christ. They are learning more and more what it means to follow, to love, and to walk in the light of Christ. Among other things, Paul encourages walking in love, just as Christ loved us.

Look carefully then how you walk, not as unwise but as wise, making the best use of the time, because the days are evil. Therefore do not be foolish, but understand what the will of the Lord is. (Ephesians 5:15–16)

We have tackled this same challenge. Our story has considered a wisdom outside of our own experiences. Our story has looked for an answer outside of our own hearts. Our story searches the will of God to inform our understanding. This means we have had to take a good hard look at our walk.

But understand what the will of the Lord is. What is the will of the Lord? How can one possibly be wise in this way? How can anyone imitate the Almighty God as a beloved child? Submission.

The humid air pressed on the still waters of the river Jordan. Only a few people had come to see John that morning, so he now reclined at the edge of the water waiting for the next baptism. From a distance, he saw a man approach with determined steps. This man boldly stepped into the murky water with a commanding intensity, very different from the other sinners that crept in slowly. There, God's most beloved Child, Jesus, stepped into the repentant water of baptism. John the Baptist was baffled when He knelt down in the water. There was nothing that Jesus had to say sorry for. And so, Jesus was not repenting for himself, rather He was baptized for the sins of others. There in the water He began His ministry of substitution. When Jesus emerged from the dirty river, God announced that He was well pleased with His Son. And Jesus perfectly submitted. Submission is what Christ does as the perfect Son. Submission is also the relationship created for God's creatures. Submission is what Christians are created to do when they love.

> Be filled with the spirit . . . submitting to one another out of reverence for Christ. Wives, to your own husbands as you do to the Lord. For the husband is the head of the wife as Christ is the head of the church, his body, of which he is the Savior. Now as the church submits to Christ, so also wives should submit to their husbands in everything. (Ephesians 5:18, 21–24)

Paul describes Christians "filled with the spirit." They are those who submit to one another. Paul continues that women belong to their own men, just as they belong to Christ. We see this relationship in Christ. He is the head of the whole church, as all believers recognize, and all submit to Him. The headship given to Christ is compared to the headship also given to man. From a Christian woman's point of view, these two roles are very similar. Man is made to be the head of woman, just as Christ is the head of His Bride, the church. Paul paints a very specific picture to women: follow the church's example, willingly submit to your head.

Just as the church submits and loves and trusts Christ, woman is made to love, trust, and submit to her husband, her father, her God. It is weaved into the very fabric of being created woman. A Christian woman gives glory and honor to her Creator by recognizing she belongs to her head. But women were not the only ones created to love.

> Husbands, love your wives, just as Christ loved the church and gave himself up for her to make her holy, cleansing her by the washing

with water through the word, and to present her to himself as a
radiant church, without stain or wrinkle or any other blemish,
but holy and blameless. In this same way, husbands ought to love
their wives as their own bodies. He who loves his wife loves himself.
After all, no one ever hated their own body, but they feed and care for
their body, just as Christ does the church—for we are members of his
body. (Ephesians 5:25–30)

Men also have been given a part in this relationship. Remember, we
are called to submit to one another because of the great and wonderful way Christ loved each of us. Yet a special and distinct love is
created for each gender. Just as we were created with complementary
bodies and purpose, both men and women are gifted complementary loves. Sacrificial love is the task of a man. Not simply flowers
and kisses, they are called to love their wives just as Christ loved
the church. Do you remember how much Christ loves His church?
He gave His life for her. He died so that she would live. He took all
the responsibility for her. He cleansed her. He made her into something beautiful, which she was not. And it continues. He nourishes
her. He cherishes her. This is a tremendous task done by the Savior
of the world. And this is how a Christian man loves his wife. A man
submits to Christ by putting on the mask of Christ for her.

This passage only reminds us again and again about the com-
pleteness of Christ's love. Christ and His church are a beautiful
example where headship and submission function properly. From
this awesome mystery, we can feebly recognize what it looks like to
be filled with the Spirit and imitate this love among one another.

"For this reason a man will leave his father and mother and be united
to his wife, and the two will become one flesh." This is a profound
mystery—but I am talking about Christ and the church. However,
each one of you also must love his wife as he loves himself, and the
wife must respect her husband. (Ephesians 5:31–33)

The mystery of Christ and His complete love is bound up in submission. He chooses to leave His Father in heaven. He lowers himself
into the dirt and grime of the prostitute, His church. He is joined to
her; they are one flesh, Christ and His church. He dies for her; she

raises with Him. They are completely inseparable. They both submit to one another in love.

Man and woman's relationship is a submission of love like this. They are joined as one flesh. He cares for her, just like she is his own body. She loves her husband, just as the church loves her Christ.

Our story from the Garden of Eden longs for this ending. Adam and Eve recognized the beauty of God's creation—they were made to love and submit to one another. Adam cried out, "Bone of my bone, flesh of my flesh!" He saw his own body in the form of his wife. The two knew that they are one flesh. But our story outside the Garden leaves us with a broken reality. The man and woman were cast out more separated than ever. She desires his power; he rules over her. Their peaceful "one flesh" is torn apart by our world of sin.

Broken, dark, tired, separate, and alone people have been wandering about in God's creation ever since. That is, until our story continues with the Boy who changed the world. Remember the Boy brings forth a beautiful bride, a restored Eve. She is a new creation, again brought forth from His side, this time marked with the blood and water trickling from the cross. The Bride is His church, and she is dressed in the blood in sacrament and in the water of baptism. The Boy gives new life to His church, His wife, His own body, His long remembered "one flesh." He gives life to you.

Yet, my daughter, we women still wander. It is dark in our world, and we don't always clearly see that the Boy, our Savior, poured life on us. Today we continue in our own stories but as if we had only an obscure picture book showing us their hidden plot. We know the victory is won. We heard He restored us to a new creation. But that truth is hidden in drops of water and a taste of a feast. The truth of peace and life is hidden in conversations about church and marriage. The answers to our struggles and strife are hidden in the words of another rather than displayed brightly before our eyes. At least for now.

The awesome truth of our story is that Jesus loved and submitted for us. He made us new. We obey and love because He does it in us. He is our flesh, and we are His. He is our sin, and we are His perfection. But the frustrating reality is we don't see this. This Ephesians text describes where we can find a glimpse of this awesome truth, right in our story today.

Men and women actually do love each other like Christ loved the church. This is how God created relationships to work. God steps into the messy emotional war between the sexes. He walks into our words and fills our hands with His gifts. He acts out love for us. Since Christ restored that broken relationship from the Garden, men and women are free to be what God created—submissive to one another.

Submission is love. Love is an action. And love submits by the work of Christ.

As with any act of love, it is not required for our eternal salvation. In Christ, you are not under compulsion to be patient and kind. There are plenty of times that I am neither patient nor kind. But these are the things that happen when love is present: actions of patience, kindness, protection, hope, and submission. Even in my best moments, I do not live up to this tall order of acting in love—Christ still forgives and loves us back. Every time, our actions fall short, and that is why that Boy walked into the house of death for us. We constantly fail in our love, and Christ wins the victory for us.

This encouragement to women and men in Ephesians 5 is nothing short of describing love that they already have. St. Paul continues in the next chapter about these relationships of love in terms of children and parents, slaves and masters. Children, love and obey your parents. Fathers, love and protect your children. Submit to one another according to who you have been created to be. Submit to one another even though your jobs are different.

Strangely enough, when we love one another and appreciate this gift God gave us, we see glimpses of the protective love of Christ. When a man guards and provides for his family, we get a taste of the peace God promised. When a woman sets her own desires aside and helps her husband, we recognized the beauty of God's restored creation. When a child listens and obeys his parents, we hear echoes of praise from the proud Almighty Father reconciled to His people once again.

We are masks of God in each other's lives. He works through our words and actions, hidden behind voices and fingers. He even uses people who do not confess His name, nor believe in His mighty deeds. The God of everything cares for you so much that He acts in the filthy dust of our messy lives. We know He is here with every good and gracious father. We feel His care with every quiet and hopeful mother. We believe His promise with each taste of bread and wine. We watch His deadly victory over sin in every baptism. We hear, feel, taste, smell, and even see the hand of God in a blurry picture of paradise.

And so the hidden mystery of Christ and His church, our story of the Boy and His Bride, looks something like a man and woman loving each other submissively. But it is true that our relationships don't always look like this. Our relationships only dimly shadow our hidden reality in Christ. But they are only a whisper of our hope and comfort in the middle of our story.

Gong and Cymbal

Our story of woman follows a storyline of love, the greatest virtue given by God. But even more, we were made to love, just as we were made to breathe. Wisdom has taught us we have been created to love one another. Wisdom moves our relationships express love to someone else. Wisdom has shaped our convictions and principles, emboldening us to love our neighbor, our spouse, our child, and our friend.

Our story began with a woman who was created to freely love God. Knit into the fibers of her being, God was the center of her praise. Hedged in by His words of life spoken all around her, God was the focus of her prayers. Bountifully displayed before her eyes, her refraining from God's Tree of Judgment was her loving worship every time she did not eat. She was not forced by God's hand to love Him, but she had no choice in the love that was first created for her.

Now we have spent many years outside of the Garden of Eden, far, far away from that unblemished relationship that freely loves our Creator. As we remember, Adam and Eve traded the spotless image of God for their own selfish and deadly version of mankind. They rejected their identity of love, which the Creator gave them as the foundation for their body and soul. Since the Garden, we are also unwilling and unable to be that loving creation He made us to be. We all have shamefully shuffled along as a seductress who has forgotten her first love, her one true God. And so, our story travels through the wilderness of a forgotten love, a forgotten identity, a forgotten story.

But, daughter, you are different now. Something amazing happened when you truly heard your story. Suddenly, you resemble someone from long ago, back from the beginning of our story.

Your restored will is loving her God, and His Word beams from your smile. Your obedient path is already alight where your feet step. Your submissive love pours out of your re-created heart. On account of Christ, you are restored in the image of God.

The most wonderful news is that you are not alone! Looking around, you see other men and women submitting to the will of their Lord. You hear about a people freely loving their Creator as they were made to do! You can even gather with these children of God who believe the promise. You can confide in believers of the story to learn and grow even more. You will find a community that will help you endure until the Bridegroom comes again.

But the shadows still remain. Even among those who believe that Christ alone made us righteous, confusion creeps in. Even among those who confess the truth from God, sometimes it is hard to hear. Even with the bright light of an eternal Word shining, darkness still lurks. Here, my daughter, is where Christ restored us to love.

> Love is patient and kind; love does not envy or boast; it is not arrogant or rude. It does not insist on its own way; it is not irritable or resentful; it does not rejoice at wrongdoing, but rejoices with the truth. Love bears all things, believes all things, hopes all things, endures all things. Love never ends. (1 Corinthians 13:4–8)

Love is acting. Love is the subject of a list of these verbs. Love is something done, not just a warm feeling. Love acts patiently. Love behaves kindly. This love is acting in you.

St. Paul shares this well-known description of love with your brothers and sisters in Christ who lived in the city of Corinth. The Corinthian church was built with men and women who gave thanks to the very same Savior we now praise. This faithful church had it problems but stands in the middle of the ancient story, just as you do today. And so, we find ourselves in the middle of this classic conversation that has captivated believers for years. How do we love one another? St. Paul has been unfolding helpful advice for the gathering of God's people, Christ's Bride, the church.

> Now you are the body of Christ and individually members of it. And God has appointed in the church first apostles, second prophets, third

teachers, then miracles, then gifts of healing, helping, administrating, and various kinds of tongues. Are all apostles? Are all prophets? Are all teachers? Do all work miracles? Do all possess gifts of healing? Do all speak with tongues? Do all interpret? (1 Corinthians 12:27–30)

The body of Christ, the church, has been given gifts. Together the people of God are one, yet each member is not the same as every other. St. Paul reminds us that we all have gifts; you have some that I don't have, and my gifts are not yours. But we are all part of the same body—working together—baptized into Christ. There are many parts of a body: legs, arms, teachers, pastors, men, women, Jews, and Greeks. All are different, all are important, and all are loved. Gifts are given by God to benefit and build up the rest of the believers. They are given to many different hands and faces to operate God's tangible love actions. Sharing these gifts with each other is how God's people walk together in hope and faith.

Different unique gifts are given to every person, but these gifts also may be misused for one's own glory and selfish purposes. Consider the gift of wealth: one man can hoard it to himself, yet another can freely give for the benefit of others. In this letter to the Corinthian church, St. Paul focuses our attention on the gift of tongues to illustrate God's action. The gift of tongues in worship is given so that the believers can hear, understand, and be built up by such an act of love; and yet this gift in this setting can also be misused.

If I speak in the tongues of men and of angels, but have not love, I am a noisy gong or a clanging cymbal. (1 Corinthians 13:1) Now, brothers and sisters, if I come to you and speak in tongues, what good will I be to you, unless I bring you some revelation or knowledge or prophecy or word of instruction? Unless you speak intelligible words with your tongue, how will anyone know what you are saying? You will just be speaking into the air.

When you come together, each of you has a hymn, or a word of instruction, a revelation, a tongue or an interpretation. Everything must be done so that the church may be built up. If anyone speaks in a tongue, two—or at the most three—should speak, one at a time, and someone must interpret. If there is no interpreter, the speaker should keep quiet in the church and speak to himself and to God. (1 Corinthians 14:6, 8, 26–28)

Daughter, God gave his Word to his people so that you would hear life. God graciously passed it from the mouth of Christ to the Christians that confess it to you now. Church is a time and a place set aside for us to gather to receive the sure gifts of Christ. The Word spoken clearly is the ultimate gift from God to us, in this assembly. So, St. Paul encourages that the Corinthians should practice their gift of tongues submissively, in the context of love.

For God is not a God of confusion but of peace. (1 Corinthians 14:33)

This place of worship is one of order and peace. The gift of tongues is good in the private realm benefitting only the one who speaks, yet this same speaking is not an act of love done selfishly, disrupting the order and peace of the public hearing of God's Word. Likewise, as we see in the next couple of verses, a woman also acts out love by remaining silent in this type of gathering. The church is being built up by her submissive love.

Women should remain silent in the churches. They are not allowed to speak, but must be in submission, as the law says. If they want to inquire about something, they should ask their own husbands at home; for it is disgraceful for a woman to speak in the church. (1 Corinthians 14:34–35)

Daughter, even though our first reaction to these hard words may be a bitter rejection of our gifts, hear Wisdom's call to love. Although the flames of equality may burn deep in your heart, try to smother them long enough to consider the bigger questions of this particular silence. The Bible speaks of many things that may be shocking to hear from our modern perspective. But Wisdom gives you more than just your experiences to trust. Wisdom guards and keeps you. Wisdom watches over you. Wisdom speaks louder than the world or your heart. Wisdom is a word outside of you that makes you understand. Wisdom saves you from death. And Wisdom continues to speak to you through the Word of God.

So this becomes the easiest and hardest thing to do in the middle of our story: simply listen to the words. Don't carry your bad experiences into the story. Don't listen to the world's screams from the shadows of liberation. Rather than change, ignore, and explain away these words of St. Paul, we will calmly soak in the syllables of these words of God. Just hear what Wisdom is saying. Hear it in the context of your great, amazing story.

> Women should remain silent in the churches. They are not allowed to speak, but must be in submission, as the law says. If they want to inquire about something, they should ask their own husbands at home; for it is disgraceful for a woman to speak in the church. (1 Corinthians 14:32–34)

In a loving order at church, women should remain silent. It's not because she is uneducated; it is not because her words are untrue; it is not because she is worth less than a man. Rather, as the Old Testament says, the *torah* of God teaches, women are in submission. She asks her own husband at home. This chapter speaks of the same submissive love we find in the broader story. However, St. Paul says even more to illustrate the gravity of this love in church; unordered speaking is disgraceful in the gathering of the congregation. It is not just disgraceful to her friends and family, but it is a disgraceful exchange of her gift from God. She should not "speak" in public worship; rather, she should bring it to her husband at home. Our minds race and wonder, what kind of female "speaking" is silenced by the Word of God? More important, what does this mean for my story?

And ever so gracefully, we are thrown back to the Garden, the beginning of our story. God created Adam and Eve as one flesh, yet bearing different gifts. God entrusted Adam with His Word: remembering, teaching, and speaking authoritatively. God formed woman to complete her husband; she was the loving ears that heard and believed God's words through the voice of her husband. She was created to freely submit to him. So here St. Paul simply reminds the Corinthians to remember the story, especially in the context of their worship.

Looking back, we want to look back to her awesome loving example, but we can only remember the shame. Satan tricked woman into stealing that fruit of power. Not only did she disgrace her God; she rose up over her husband. She fell into the unbelieving trap of the Evil One. Sadly, even in hindsight, we like the loud and dirty way she forgot how to submit. We cheer her on to bite into her independence. We stand up and selfishly scream her praises in the middle of God's quiet sanctuary.

Daughter, here in the New Testament, we also are tempted to hate the Word of God. We feel the rub of inequality, the sting of something not right. We dream of exceptional situations where this Word cannot possibly apply: in the absence of men, in the face of unloving or untruthful men, in the most obscure places and times, anywhere and anything to make these words not say what they intend. We ignore these words as a culturally bound teaching, not applying to our life right now. We welcome Satan's twists and lies when it comes to verses like this. Something makes us very uncomfortable about the word "submission," and we do our very best to deflect these words of God. But if we just listen, if we remember our beautiful story of creation, honor, and love, then we can recognize what it is we really hate about this word "submission."

We hate that it is hard. We hate that we don't submit, and we don't even want to do it. We hate that men have different jobs that they don't even do well. We hate that our relationships are broken. We hate trying to submit and being totally disappointed. We hate our experience with submission.

Rightly so. We hate those reminders of our sin. We hate the things that tell us, "No, you are not good." We hate the mirror and the guide that shows us where to walk and shows us how badly we do it. This knowledge of good and evil that Eve won for us with her shiny apple only left us with things we hate. It left us with a law that we have learned we can never live up to. It left us in the terrible little house on the corner, as a knowledgeable seductress creating her own personal house of pleasures, to hide from the words she hates to hear.

But our story does not end with the death of this disobedient woman. Our Lord Jesus Christ quietly, submissively stood in the path of her loud indiscretion. Jesus was clothed her screams and cries. And God blamed Him instead of her.

Neither does our story end with the bitter heart of the enlightened woman. Our Lord Jesus Christ swallowed every bite of lawless
fruit so that no one else would be able to eat anymore. Woman's sto-
len taste of knowledge pinned Jesus to the cross. God poisoned and
killed Him instead.

Punished for our knowledge, raised with a newly created body,
Jesus is the good, obedient, perfect Child for you. Killed for your
speech, resurrected with a calm quiet smile, Jesus loves patiently,
kindly, and submissively for you. Our story daily breathes in the submission of our Savior. Our story tastes the feast to come given by our
Lord. He welcomes His beautiful, holy Bride out of the pit of death
and places you back at His warm protective side.

Because you were created to love, reconciled and renewed by
Christ . . .

> Women should remain silent in the churches. They are not allowed
> to speak, but must be in submission, as the law says. If they want to
> inquire about something, they should ask their own husbands at
> home . . . (1 Corinthians 14:34–35)

This is your gift of love to your church.

Daughter, even in my own search for understanding, this story
began to take shape. Keeping the short digression about women in the
same conversation as speaking in misunderstood tongues, suddenly I
could recognize St. Paul's emphasis on good order. I regularly go to a
church service that has a beginning, a middle, and an end. It is clear
when the pastor will speak those life-giving words of forgiveness. I
also know when I get to eat and drink for the forgiveness of my sins.
There is time for reflection; there is an opportunity to praise. There is
a good order to the worship life of my church. Now if people started
jumping up in the middle of service yelling unintelligible things, this
would make it a hard for me to hear the gifts of Christ. The unruly
speaking would be distracting, misunderstood, and in competition
with the life-giving Word of Christ. Those disrupting the order would
be selfishly drawing attention, unlovingly ignoring the others around
them. Their gifts would be misused in the greater assembly, among
the body of Christ.

Just as it is shameful to destroy the good order among prophets and tongue speakers, it is also not acceptable to destroy the good order of creation among man and woman. This good order in worship is for the purpose of building up others in love. Especially in this public place, keeping the order of a head and one in submission is an act of love and edification in church.

> A woman should learn in quietness and full submission. I do not permit a woman to teach or to assume authority over a man; she must be quiet. For Adam was formed first, then Eve. And Adam was not the one deceived; it was the woman who was deceived and became a sinner. But women will be saved through childbearing—if they continue in faith, love and holiness with propriety. (1 Timothy 2:11-15)

Here we find a bit more about the central issue of "speaking" in a worship setting. St. Paul writes this letter to a young leader in the church, Timothy. This letter is from pastor to pastor, not directly to people in a church. Paul's advice is for Timothy's instruction as he cares for God's people. So Paul begins this letter with the Gospel message, "*(God) wants all people to be saved and to come to a knowledge of the truth. For there is one God and one mediator between God and mankind, the man Christ Jesus, who gave himself as a ransom for all people*" (1 Timothy 2:4-6). This is the clear Word given to all Christians, Christ's ransom for all. Paul continues by describing the response of a church who loves each other with their God-given gifts. Both men and women hear, learn, and participate in this knowledge. But again, both men and women have particular gifts in the gathering of the people of God.

> I desire then that in every place the men should pray, lifting holy hands without anger or quarreling; likewise also that women should adorn themselves in respectable apparel, with modesty and self-control, not with braided hair and gold or pearls or costly attire, but with what is proper for women who profess godliness—with good works. A woman should learn in quietness and full submission. I do not permit a woman to teach or to assume authority over a man; she must be quiet. (1 Timothy 2:8-12)

Paul first focuses on the men; Christians pray together and do it without anger or fighting. Every church that confesses Christ will find these men—praying, lifting holy hands without anger or quarreling. This is who they have been created to be, sharing their gifts with one another in love as faithful believers in the Gospel. Next Paul focuses his attention on the women of the congregation in the description of the faithful. First, women wear good deeds instead of showy outfits. Second, they learn silently. Third, women do not do certain authoritative things in church: teach or have authority over a man. This also fits who they also have been created to be.

This serves as a peaceful picture of God's people. What a harmonious image. Every man praying together without strife? Women who don't care what they look like but can't do enough good deeds for others? What kind of a world possibly looks like this? Women are modest and loving; they do not draw selfish attention to themselves but focus on the Word of God. Women ask their husband about things at home for the sake of good order. Women are content to not teach men or have authority over them. Women fully support the ones created to serve as "head" to teach and lead the congregation. Every man and woman loves with their own gifts, without dissention and strife in this serene vision of worship. But this looks nothing like our loud and confused churches.

In our ancient story, the only time we can remember this gentle loving church was a very long time ago. Again, our tale races back to the Garden of Eden. Adam spoke the words of God; his wife listened. They lived peacefully in the blessings of God's good creation. Except for that one time . . . when the woman was deceived to speak authoritatively. In the Garden, neither did she lovingly submit to her husband nor to her God. She did not use her gifts for the sake of love as she was created to do. Rather, she listened to her selfish desires and her prideful logic. She adorned herself with the deadly riches of disobedient knowledge. This letter to Timothy only continues to tell the great story from the Garden. Not from the whim of Paul's opinion, nor from an ever-changing cultural tradition, rather the Word of God from creation speaks about the good order of man and woman.

Lest we believe that this is simply a time-bound reality, lest we think that these verses do not say something about our worship today, St. Paul grounds his words about women in the forgotten story that applies to every creation of God.

For Adam was formed first, then Eve. And Adam was not the one deceived; it was the woman who was deceived and became a sinner. (1 Timothy 2:13–14)

We begin with God's action. He formed Adam first. He made Eve to follow. First in God's "very good" plan of creation, He blessed His creatures with an order. Unlike cultural traditions that may evolve and change, the gift of man and woman's creation has not changed. Adam was created to lead. He was formed first. He named all the animals, including the very bone-and-flesh human before his eyes. He was created to speak out loud God's words in their young worship setting. He was personally given the command of God to preach and be the mouthpiece of the Almighty God. He was created to protect the very flesh that followed him, his wife.

Woman was created to love. She was formed to correspond to him; the same flesh, yet very different. She was part of Adam's own side, and she was one flesh with him. She was given a man from which she gladly heard and learned the words of God. When the woman was deceived by the Devil, her protector was not the one who decided their fate. When woman took a bite of the deadly fruit, her pastor's words were not guiding her. When woman seized Adam's gifts and spoke in agreement with the Devil, we all became sinners.

The Evil One tricked woman into a position that was not given to her in the Garden. She was led to forget that her gifts in creation were good. She listened to the lies of the Devil about knowledge and prestige and satisfaction. But she didn't remember to trust her husband. And she most certainly forgot the words of her God.

This ancient story Paul tells reveals the unchanging truth of God's creation in God's church of believers. Man is still created to lead and speak in the church today. Woman is still created to love and submit in the greater assembly of God's people. The identity of man and woman has not changed, except now we actively rebel against the gifts He gave us.

But women will be saved through childbearing—if they continue in faith, love and holiness with propriety. (1 Timothy 2:15)

Yet our story moved on. Through a house of death, raised to a new life, women are saved. Women do not bear the curse of sin anymore. Women will be saved by the very thing God created them to do: have children. Women are restored beautiful creations, who look like what God created. Only the female creature can bear children, as their bodies were created to do. And women are restored to life by a very particular childbearing: the birth of a Christ.

Adam preached this hope in the newly broken world, in the beginning. For the sake of both man and woman, he told her, "You will be mother of all the living." That is what Eve means. From the womb of the sinner, childbirth will save her. This childbirth will save us all. This Child will crush the head of the Evil One. He will undo all the terrible strife that infects the whole creation. This Child was the very same Boy who quietly napped in an unknown manger. This Child was the very same Boy who silently walked into the house of the adulteress who was possessed by the Evil One. This Child was the very same Boy who lovingly submitted to His Father and was raised to everlasting life. Eve's promise lives. Woman's promise lives. Our promise lives. Women, and all of us, will be saved through childbearing.

Creatures of God, we now resemble what He created. Yet at the same time, we are scarred, timid, and skittish because of our terrible experiences, the unhelpful world, and that nasty Devil. Since our beginning in the Garden, women have endured thousands of years of pain and angst. But since the victory at the little dark house on the corner, we have also been recreated to love perfectly, peacefully, and submissively. We exist in the overlapping chapters of the same great story, both trudging through darkness of sin and walking freely in the light of the Promised Child.

Wisdom shares her glimpse of the peaceful Christian church, living boldly in the freedom of Christ, loving each other in extremely considerate ways.

Daughter, your loving submission is cast in a whole new light. If a woman's love for neighbor is shown by keeping God's order at church, don't you want to care for your neighbor? Of course you want to help. Your quiet submissive gifts display your love. These are encouraged just as praying, building up, and keeping gibberish to oneself. We all use our gifts, even those given in our creation as woman, to benefit our family in Faith.

When Wisdom taught me this forgotten story once again, I began to realize I didn't want to teach or have authority over a man at church. I began to love the gift of creation God created for us. I could finally see that a woman's submission is a gift to the faithful. But, daughter, there is a danger with every gift. To require it, to impose it, to bind a heart to do certain works: you lose Wisdom. When you begin to hope and trust in your own ability to love and obey, beware. If you focus your own eyes upon the acts of silence among women instead on the external Word of Christ, beware.

And so, my daughter, here you will not find a specific compilation of ways to submit quietly. You will not find an excursus on when and where to teach. This story is not for you to use as a checklist of good works. This story is not for you to create a perfect world for yourself and others here on earth. Rather, it is a story of your real identity. Simply believing your story produces inevitable gifts of love that flow from God. You cannot by your own reason or strength believe in Jesus Christ or come to Him; but the Holy Spirit has called you by the Gospel, enlightens you with His gifts, and sanctifies and keeps you in the true faith. Your actions are no longer from you, and even your silence in love is His.

Your service to others, even in church, flows from this new identity. You have been recreated by Wisdom, free to love submissively. Wisdom speaks into your ears and rushes through your veins. Our questions about teaching, leading, ushering, reading, speaking, and ministering are all colored with the blood of Christ. But you are also forgiven when you do not love, freed from punishment. Your identity does not change with your actions. Your sinful ignorant past was killed at the house on the corner, when the Boy died for you. Christ has already dressed you in His white wedding clothes. Right now, you are His beloved Bride, and nothing can snatch you away from His side. Right now, you have been made new, and you remember you were never on your own.

All of our practical questions about "what to do now" begin and end with the remembered story. Our submissive love may even act differently in various times and places, but there are parts of the story that never change. We are women who all confess the same truth about our story. We are women created in a special way by God. We are sinful women redeemed by Christ. This is not my own wisdom, these are not my actions of love, but this is the Wisdom of Christ.

> For through the law I died to the law, so that I might live to God. I have been crucified with Christ. It is no longer I who live, but Christ who lives in me. (Galatians 2:19–20)

Christ loves patiently; Christ loves kindly. He does not envy; He does not boast; He is not proud. Christ does not dishonor others; He is not self-seeking; He is not easily angered; He keeps no record of wrongs. Christ does not delight in evil but rejoices with the truth. He always protects, always trusts, always hopes, always perseveres. And Christ lives in you.

This is your story.

Top-Down Organization

Wisdom guides us through our story with a resurrected appreciation for our gifts. She reminds us that God created us to love and live in a relationship with Him. She reminds us that God gave us men to work His protective love in our lives. Wisdom focuses our story directly on the Savior that clothed us in a righteous wedding dress embellished with love.

Daughter, Wisdom remembers you from the beginning of creation. But I can remember when you were just a little toddler not long ago. You loved hats. I remember picking out the most beautiful jumpsuits and church dresses, only to be topped with a cute little hat that matched. I can still almost feel the tiny blue cotton hat with the dainty pink flower print. Because of your surprising compliance, hats were a natural part of your wardrobe, even as a baby.

This is not a normal reaction to such restrictive headgear. Most sweet little ones tear the beautiful hats from their heads, throw them on the ground, and laugh at the new game they have discovered! And of course, it makes sense not to be comfortable in such attire. When you are young and simple, hats seem to be an unnecessary burden. Hats seem like they should be for the older and more dignified crowd. They seem like they should be reserved for special occasions. They seem to have gone out of style.

What if I told you, sweet daughter, that once upon a time your hat was more than just a fashion statement? It has served Christians as a symbol of a greater truth. Since we live in a world where we cannot always see the things that we believe, our daily lives turn into great metaphors for the secret things of faith. One such symbol was a hat. It confessed a truth about men and women beyond what our eyes would show us.

> But I want you to understand that the head of every man is Christ, the head of a wife is her husband, and the head of Christ is God. (1 Corinthians 11:3)

Our story travels through the city of Corinth many years ago, among a people who had a tradition of involving hats in their worship expression. The men and women went to pray and praise God; men went uncovered, women covered their head. St. Paul wrote this letter to the Corinthians concerning many issues—namely, to endure in the Christian Faith that they had been handed. He praises his brothers and sisters for following his instruction about some specific traditions in their church. He continues by teaching the Corinthians more about these good and honorable traditions. Now, daughter, before you dismiss this all as a dated trend among a foreign people, Wisdom calls you to hear this convincing argument that actually means something in our story today. The metaphor of hats is speaking about a greater reality, and it applies to every man and woman of every age. It means something for you.

> But I want you to understand that the head of every man is Christ, the head of a wife is her husband, and the head of Christ is God. (1 Corinthians 11:3)

This is the greater truth that the Corinthians confessed by observing the tradition of headcoverings. They were already doing this practice, and Paul wanted them to understand why it was a good tradition. He explains it so they understand the foundation for their tradition. The following discussion about Corinthian church tradition is an example of this greater truth acted out among these Christians. This foundation, which is true for all Christians at all times, is the starting point for the headcovering tradition to follow.

> Every man who prays or prophesies with his head covered dishonors his head, but every wife who prays or prophesies with her head uncovered dishonors her head, since it is the same as if her head were

shaven. For if a wife will not cover her head, then she should cut her hair short. But since it is disgraceful for a wife to cut off her hair or shave her head, let her cover her head. (1 Corinthians 11:4–6)

The Corinthian practice in worship involves a headcovering for both sexes. A man must not wear one. A woman must keep her head covered. Shame resulted when the tradition was not kept. Although it could seem like women are praying and prophesying in the church, Paul's emphasis right now is not on her speaking, but rather on the manner of headcovering, and what that practice says without her words. He addresses a woman's voice in church in chapter 14. Here he tells the Corinthians, both man and woman, to come before the Lord, yet both man and woman approach differently.

Now I know what you may be thinking. What does this have to do with me? It is not my tradition to pray with my head covered or uncovered. Why should I care about what Paul has to say to these people? You are right. Our traditions are different. Today in American Christianity, we do not see much of this practice. But a headcovering meant something to the Corinthian people. Their actions here said something about their lives, their honor, and even their spouses. A woman praying without a headcovering looked like a man, or possibly even a prostitute. Her clothing and hair spoke just as much as her words to everyone around her. She publicly humiliated and shamed her husband by casting aside the tradition. Likewise, men praying with a headcovering looked like all the other covered up women. It was a visible disregard for the truth of his responsibility to his wife and the church. Shame before God resulted in Corinth when the actions of men and women spoke out against what was true. These words also speak to us when we hear about the greater truth behind the Corinthian tradition of headcovering. In our story even today, shame follows when our actions speak out against what God tells us is true.

For a man ought not to cover his head, since he is the image and glory of God, but woman is the glory of man. For man was not made from woman, but woman from man. Neither was man created for woman, but woman for man. That is why a wife ought to have a symbol of authority on her head, because of the angels. Nevertheless, in the Lord woman is not independent of man nor man of woman; for as woman was made from man, so man is now born of woman. And all things are from God. (1 Corinthians 11:7–12)

Headcovering seeks to confess God's good order of man and woman, given in Genesis 1 and 2, back at the beginning of our story. We hear again that the head of every man is Christ, and the head of a wife is her husband. Headcovering is a visual display of God's created order. Men and women here in Corinth actually dress as God's creations. They are given these gifts by God, and man and woman happily reflect these gifts in the tradition of headcovering. Paul reminds us of the creation account that every man and woman can relate to. Woman comes from the side of a man. She was created second for a specific purpose. The story recalls she was created from the man to help the man. Man was given the unique position of authority among all of God's earthly creatures to name and have dominion over. They are completely distinct from one another.

But Paul also emphasizes they are not separate from each other. Man and woman need each other. There is no independence in God's good garden. They are indeed one flesh. "Male and female he created them" (Genesis 1:27). Since they were the first parents to all people, both were essential to procreate. All men since Adam were born from Eve. He needs her to live on from generation to generation. And ultimately, the Savior of the world would come from a woman. The beauty and mystery of this head and submissive relationship is highlighted beautifully where the man and women are completely unique and, at the same time, completely dependent on one another.

Judge for yourselves: is it proper for a wife to pray to God with her head uncovered? (1 Corinthians 11:13)

So, my daughter, what do you think? Paul explains the background of the tradition and argues that it is helpful for understanding a timeless unchanging truth about men and women. Do you believe this truth—that God created woman from the side of a man? Headcoverings were a visible, physical representation of the creation of man and woman. In good order, this was a reasonable and helpful tradition rooted in a beautiful confession of creation.

However, when this tradition becomes empty and misunderstood, it just becomes another law to follow and break. When this practice is required of women and men, it moves from the joyful confession of creation to the oppressive law of good order. All meaningful traditions teeter on this delicate line between helpful, focused worship and binding, crushing law. It begins as a good and faithful expression of God's Word. But when our sinful lives crash into these good works, things get confused. Women are bothered by their hat, women take pride in their hat, women rebel against their hat, women join the faithful hat club, women forget the reason they ever owned a hat in the first place. What begins as an edifying pattern of worship can quickly be disfigured into a meaningless mess.

To complicate matters, this is not even a tradition with which we are very familiar. Most men and women in our churches do not observe headcoverings as an expression of God's created order. More troubling, in our present culture, we are shocked to even hear that God has created an order for man and woman. We are led to believe that we are "created equal," that we are not really different at all, and that submission means that women have been unjustly oppressed. Even worse, we are beginning to experience and even accept the plague of gender confusion in our mixed-up society. Males are changing themselves into females, women are claiming gender neutrality, and there are even people that are so blinded to the gifts given in creation that they somehow have chosen both. Our world can't hear the old story of a man and woman carefully created. In the middle of this noise, it is also hard for us to remember the part where God gifted His people with an order. But despite our modern lack of any headship and submissive tradition, the truth of God's creation remains the same.

So do you believe what God has revealed through His Word?

> But I want you to understand that the head of every man is Christ, the head of a wife is her husband, and the head of Christ is God. (1 Corinthians 11:3)

Our beautiful Garden story attests to this, and our ancient brothers and sisters in Corinth also attest to this. Even your heart cries out for this. Truthfully, you have been created for another. You were not meant to wander in the desert, outside of Eden, alone.

So even if we do not practice our confession of His created gifts for us, if we do not wear our headcovering to honor our Creator, we still believe His Word. Our traditions may not be as bold, but we will still show the respect and love for our head, our husband, and our God. Our identity still confesses the great truth of men and women, even if our hats do not.

> Does not nature itself teach you that if a man wears long hair it is a disgrace for him, but if a woman has long hair, it is her glory? For her hair is given to her for a covering. (1 Corinthians 11:14–15)

Although trends and fashions change, Paul refers to a characteristic that has been generally observed. Men naturally have shorter hair than women. Of course, this is not a hard and fast rule or a law that must be kept. Rather it is an appeal to observing God's creation. The length of hair covering that God gives His people corresponds to this good tradition of headcovering in worship. Longer hair is given to women as a beautiful asset, but it also serves as a headcovering. Likewise, men who have long hair may be mistaken for a woman—because that is the general nature of things. Even God's gifts of a creature's appearance can reflect the order of headship and subordination, headcovering or not. But the next verse puts this whole discussion in perspective for us.

> If anyone is inclined to be contentious, we have no such practice, nor do the churches of God. (1 Corinthians 11:16)

This final verse, my daughter, is where the Law is crushed by Gospel. Tradition, good practice, rules, and order can be helpful. They can bloom from a beautiful understanding of the gifts we have been given by God. They can train us to believe the words of God with our actions. The law can shape, guide, and teach us amazing things. But this Law also kills. It lies in wait to catch you when you fail. It judges and measures your every move. It traps you into believing rules and traditions will somehow make you a better person. It crushes you to nothing, because you can never finish this Law.

But our story is the not bound in the Law. Our story is saturated with Gospel. Gospel is the good news of a gift of life in the face of the death we deserve. Gospel is the good news of the Boy defeating evil so that His Bride would walk as a new creation. Gospel is the good news that traditions, practice, and the even the Law of God does not hold us captive.

This is an extremely important distinction in understanding who you are. Christ has completely taken control of your destiny. He did all the work: the perfect life, the death, the resurrection, and the raising of you as well. There is not one little thing left for any of us to claim as our own good work. Life is freely given, unexpectedly shouted into your ears, because He carried you from the little house of death on the corner.

But consider the whole picture. What does Christ carry away from sin, death, and the Devil? In His arms is a breathtaking Bride, spotless and clean, covered by His mercy. What she is wearing matters—it is the garment of salvation. She didn't go shopping to pick it out. She didn't decide white was the flattering color. She was clothed, passively, even against her will. He violently made her into something beautiful. And now she just is.

So now, she looks different. She looks like what she was created to be. She looks like that calm woman in the Garden, the one before the Serpent's deceit, before the terrible pain and strife, before the Law of God killed. On account of Christ, she now looks like the woman God made.

In our daily reality, even though headcoverings confess a true and profound reality about the creation of men and women, even though headcoverings continue to teach men and women about the generous gifts of their Creative God, even though headcoverings proclaims order in the churches and in the home, this is not the important part of the story. Headcoverings are simply a confession of a greater truth for the sake of love.

Women and men showed their love to one another by honoring this tradition. As with other expressions of the Law (what to do and not do), actions like these are greatly helpful to your neighbor. But if someone wants to fight about it, well, there is no such practice. Because the practice is not what is of value. The Law does not define us. Our freedom in the face of this action of love comes from Christ alone.

Our battles today are less often about traditional headcoverings and more often about traditional "roles" such as where men and women work. Observing the current culture, if a woman stays at home, she is understood to honor her head. If a man stays home, he may be accused of not leading as he should. While there may be good reasons to support each side of the argument, and there might be sound advice to helpfully love one another in a certain place rather than another, the traditions we assume do not define our identity. What we do or where we work does not provide freedom. Christ living and dying for those at home and at work restores our broken relationship, no matter where we are.

We, as redeemed women, will not be judged if we cover our heads or shave our heads. We are free from condemnation if we work full time or stay at home. It is not this practice that saves us or makes us into better Christians. Our hope rests only on Jesus—His death for our sin, His resurrection for our new life. We are dead to the cage of the Law or the restrictions of any tradition.

So, my daughter, what do you want to do?

This question is where our neatly defined traditions get awfully messy. While we can all make a good case for what actions and traditions best represent God's creation, this will always fall short and someone will always be contentious. Freedom from the Law is quite scary. We cannot control what this beautiful Bride of Christ will do. Her actions will filter into our world in a thousand different manifestations. But we can only trust that she loves who she is: the woman Christ restored her to be.

> But I want you to understand that the head of every man is Christ, the head of a wife is her husband, and the head of Christ is God. (1 Corinthians 11:3)

This verse is not telling us to do anything. This is simply describing the story as we have heard it from the beginning. God created His creatures in a special relationship—God, Christ, husband, wife. Believing this story and loving this story makes us want to live this story. For the Corinthian church, they believed, loved, and expressed it by their headcovering. The tradition was an expression of love for God's created order, and a love for His gifts to them as man and woman.

You, also, believe and love this story. Daughter, you were made, and then made again, for love. But Christ dressed you in freedom to express your love by wearing hats, or not. You are free to stay home to help or go to work at the bar. You are free to vote at the church meetings or make Jell-O salad for the potluck. You are free to confess your created identity. I just want you to understand that the head of every man is Christ, the head of a wife is her husband, and the head of Christ is God. If this is the gift of who you are, judge for yourself: what do you want to do?

The Groaning

My daughter, this is the point where most of us wanted this story to begin: advice for our own lives and guidance for our less-than-perfect situations. I know that you have been patiently waiting with your real questions and heartache. Politely reading along until the practical how-to entered the conversation. But the real question looms over our heads now. What happens when our relationships don't follow this story line?

Up until now, we have heard the story of a woman created, loved, saved, and preserved. We heard the story of a beautiful relationship of love and headship and submission. We heard the call to serve quietly. We expect our men to love us graciously. Up until now, our story has been in the realm of ideals. This storybook romance has been no more than a distant fairytale. Our God and His hidden reality whisper to us in metaphor and breathe hopeful shadows into our actual lives. But this is where our ancient story smashes into our everyday.

Daughter, beware; this is the place where most of our misguided lies are born—because we believe at the center of it all, the most relevant story begins with me.

Wisdom exposes your true and beautiful story that did not begin with you. We hear that woman was created, loved, and redeemed as a new creature, but we do not see that. Right now, we are experiencing a much darker story in the span of our lifetime. Today we are seeing the effects of sin. We are feeling the pain in childbearing. We are struggling for power when men lord it over us and women fight against submission. We are experiencing real pain when men don't care for women as Christ loved the church. We are totally alone even when God says it is not good. We are single, we are separated, we are divorced, we are independent, and we are unhappy. The hope of creation, the blessing of marriage, the great story of a new life seems like an imaginary fairytale if we are honest about the raw reality in which we live.

But Wisdom calls out to you to remember your story—especially when it is hard.

> Live as people who are free, not using your freedom as a cover-up for evil, but living as servants of God. Honor everyone. Love the brotherhood. Fear God. Honor the emperor. (1 Peter 2:16–17)

And so, Peter's words are simple and bold in these bleak days. Be who you were created to be, who Christ restored you to be.

> Be subject . . . with all respect, not only to the good and gentle but also to the unjust. For this is a gracious thing, when, mindful of God, one endures sorrows while suffering unjustly. (1 Peter 2:18–19)

Yet St. Peter takes up the terrible collision of our ancient story with our messy life. It isn't pretty. It isn't easy. It isn't a perfect picture of what we know to be true. He encourages us, in fact, in the places where things are not right. Unjust rulers and forces will try to impose on you. Terrible lords will try to scare you away from your freedom. They will mock you and hurt you and tempt you to believe God's Word is not enough.

> Likewise, wives, be subject to your own husbands, so that even if some do not obey the word, they may be won without a word by the conduct of their wives, when they see your respectful and pure conduct. Do not let your adorning be external—the braiding of hair and the putting on of gold jewelry, or the clothing you wear—but let your adorning be the hidden person of the heart with the imperishable beauty of a gentle and quiet spirit, which in God's sight is very precious. For this is how the holy women who hoped in God used to adorn themselves, by submitting to their own husbands, as Sarah obeyed Abraham, calling him lord. And you are her children, if you do good and do not fear anything that is frightening. (1 Peter 3:1–6)

Be comforted, my daughter: there are women who have been a part of this story long before you and me. Generations of women have heard the call of Wisdom, and they believed her words. These girls found themselves in the midst of confusing and difficult situations, yet they trusted in a protective head, trusted in a God who loved them, and trusted in the continuation of our ancient story.

The long dusty road led Sarah to Gerar. The country was unfamiliar, and she had no idea what to expect from this town she now approached. Every step closer to the little village, she strained her ears to listen for strange men approaching. Her stomach twisted in fear for what this place would do to her and her husband, Abraham.

Sarah, our sister in faith, believed this story in spite of her own hard circumstances. Her husband, Abraham, was a gift. He protected her; he loved her; he was the hands and mouth of the hidden God for her. And yes, Abraham was a sinner. There were times when Sarah was afraid. There were times when she was confused and mad. There were times when she thought it was just too hard to continue, but she hoped in God. She looked at her husband and treated him as the mask of God.

Earlier in their journey together, Sarah was told that she would bear a child. Both she and her husband were very old. Yet God kept His promise to her, despite the dismal and unlikely circumstances. Sarah trusted in God's good and gracious gifts. She believed Abraham's words and God's promises. She expected Him to care for her, even when she was unsure of her future. She hoped in God and beautifully reflected the woman that God created in the Garden.

Years later, a much younger girl was surprised by unfortunate circumstances. Unmarried, promised to another, she discovered she was pregnant. How humiliating it was when her friends whispered. How heartbreaking it was when she had to leave her home, dishonored. But the mother of our Lord, Mary, hoped in God. She believed this story and said, "I am a servant of the Lord; let it be to me according to your word."

Sadly, our world today would tell Sarah and Mary that they were wrong. It would counsel these girls to seek their own happiness. It would chastise them for not speaking their minds. It would empower them to fight against the injustices they experienced. But Sarah and Mary hoped in God. They held tightly to the ancient story that Wisdom revealed to them. Because they trusted their sure identity before God, they could freely submit in the middle of these terrible circumstances.

This is the "precious adornment" that St. Peter encourages for women: simply believing your story. We know from our own experiences that dresses, high heels, braids, pearls, and lipstick do not make up the essence of a woman. Rather, she was created purposefully. She was created beautifully. She was created to help. She was created to love quietly, gently, submissively, and fearlessly. This is just how the women of God happen to look.

> Be subject . . . with all respect, not only to the good and gentle but also to the unjust. For this is a gracious thing, when, mindful of God, one endures sorrows while suffering unjustly. For what credit is it if, when you sin and are beaten for it, you endure? But if when you do good and suffer for it you endure, this is a gracious thing in the sight of God. (1 Peter 2:18–20)

You, my daughter, are a conqueror, but at the very same time, you suffer unjustly. Christ has loved you and crowned you as His beloved Bride, but you still struggle in the valley of death. At the very same time that you belong in the great story of the victorious Savior, you still live in a broken reality. The difference is that you know of the two worlds in which you walk. However, you now know which world is true and eternal.

So your love looks a little crazy. You can love even when love is undeserved. You can love the good and gentle, but you can also love the aberrations of creation. You can love the unfaithful. You can love a liar and a cheat. You can love the one who does not obey the Word. But how can you possibly do that? As with the rest of our great tale, our story always flows through Christ's love.

> For to this you have been called, because Christ also suffered for you, leaving you an example, so that you might follow in his steps. He committed no sin, neither was deceit found in his mouth. When he was reviled, he did not revile in return; when he suffered, he did not threaten, but continued entrusting himself to him who judges justly. He himself bore our sins in his body on the tree, that we might die to

sin and live to righteousness. By his wounds you have been healed.
(1 Peter 2:21–24)

This is who we are, daughter. We are dead to sin, and we live to righteousness because He raised us to this new life. Just like you were created female, not by your own choice, but the gracious gift of God, likewise, He recreated you to live the life He made for you. Precious new life, a Bride steps forth from the house of death. He took up all of her sin and shame. He became one flesh with His unfaithful people. She is dressed in the white garments of perfection because she steps forth as one flesh with her Bridegroom. They are one—dead to sin, alive in righteousness. And so your life looks like Christ's, silent suffering, eternal life, and all. For this you have been called.

The easy book to write would tell you how to avoid this suffering. The bestseller would let you know what steps to take to get out of a destructive relationship. The popular story would redefine a woman with independence. We all have lovely friends trapped in suffocating lives, and our lips itch to give them advice to resolve everything for themselves. But this story is not one of lies of dishonest hope. Other false teachers want us to avoid the cross of Christ. Other gospels want us to ignore the life given to us and create a better one. But those other endings are not the beautiful eternal story of Christ and His Bride.

The death of a Boy brings us new life. Although today we linger between the pages of the Garden and Eternity, we know those wounds have healed us. Even though we are still caught up in injustice and unfortunate events, we can freely and boldly live today as a new creation. This is how St. Peter can encourage women to love their husbands, even now when we still live in the present darkness.

Our love is no different than before, except it is among the evil that still walks beside us. We submit freely, not because our lives are happy homemaker perfect. Nor do we submit because we are under compulsion to do so. Rather, our life joined to Christ submits freely in the most terrible of circumstances. And of course, this does not just apply to women. Both men and women are made to love each other, in the worst of times.

Likewise, wives, be subject to your own husbands, so that even if some do not obey the word, they may be won without a word by the

conduct of their wives, when they see your respectful and pure conduct. (1 Peter 3:1)

Specifically, this verse addresses wives and their own husbands. It
is a personal and intimate love only she can display. It's not about
women in general submitting to the mass of men. Rather, it is the
gentle and sacrificial love of a humble Christ who was even killed
for a loving submission. Back in Ephesians, our men are called to
love like Christ, sacrificing everything to save her life. Likewise,
here in 1 Peter, women are called to love like Christ especially when
it's hard.

What we realize quickly is that hardship meets us more than
not in this lifetime. Most of us have never even seen a relationship
that loves like this: a man who leads patiently and justly, a woman
who submits happily and quietly. We long to be in this story, the one
that works out beautifully as God intended. We want to be the happy
creations of a God who loves them. We seek an unblemished relationship between creatures who walk through this world together.
We are almost too afraid to imagine it is true.

We are scared because we know too well that men don't obey
the Word. We know women won't listen. We've lived in our world
long enough to experience heartbreak, tears, death, and aloneness.
We live in destructive relationships. We walk alongside sinners who
don't believe. We have been taught to care for ourselves outside of a
loving father, husband, or head. We are put in lives of pain, and we
long for relief.

> For we know that the whole creation has been groaning together in
> the pains of childbirth until now. And not only the creation, but we
> ourselves, who have the firstfruits of the Spirit, groan inwardly as
> we wait eagerly for adoption as sons, the redemption of our bodies.
> (Romans 8:22–23)

It gets even worse. Our visible disappointments are not only
in relationships; even the water and the trees cry out to their
Creator. All of creation was torn apart by sin. Trees and plants
do not produce fruit like they once did. Weeds and dust choke
out the life God created for His earth. Water poisons and floods

communities. It hides in drought and kills the people that God created. Our bodies were crafted to be fed by the gifts of creation: food and water. Yet these days, even creation groans and dies alongside us.

It's not right! Men hurt women. Trees wilt and die. Women yearn to be alone. This world hates men protecting daughters, wives, and widows. Trusting hearts are abandoned by those whom were created to love. This culture entices women to get a degree and a job to measure their worth. We are forced to choose between degrees of evil for the sake of our children. The righteous suffer, fall away, and die. These are perversions of God's good creation. And we live right in the middle of it. Sadly, we now realize that this ancient story is not our self-help solution. It is not a ten-step plan to success. Our story is simply our history, our present reality, and our future. It is just who we are, our identity, even now when the mountains are crumbling around us. Rightly so, we cry out for justice. We groan and cry out with our sin-sick world. We pray to our Lord to end to the pain. Exhausted and weak, we settle for fractions of the beautiful life we know we were created for. But we still hope in the story that we can only hear with our ears.

Daughter, it is so easy to forget our story. It is possible that we don't even believe it's true. The suffering and unfairness cloud the future. The incredible story of our hope to come—right now, it can't be seen. But this is not the end of the story. There is a hope that we can only dimly see.

> For I consider that the sufferings of this present time are not worth comparing with the glory that is to be revealed to us. For the creation waits with eager longing for the revealing of the sons of God. For the creation was subjected to futility, not willingly, but because of him who subjected it, in hope that the creation itself will be set free from its bondage to corruption and obtain the freedom of the glory of the children of God. For we know that the whole creation has been groaning together in the pains of childbirth until now. And not only the creation, but we ourselves, who have the firstfruits of the Spirit, groan inwardly as we wait eagerly for adoption as sons, the redemption of our bodies. For in this hope we were saved. Now hope that is seen is not hope. For who hopes for what he sees? But

if we hope for what we do not see, we wait for it with patience. (Romans 8:18–25)

We continue to watch for everything to be made new and peaceful and fruitful once again. We expect God to show us the work He has finished completely in Christ. We hold on with anticipation.

The ending to our story is yet to come.

Confidently Ever After

This is your story. You now know who you are and from where you came. Even though the start of this tale was so long ago, your story continues. And the end is almost here.

This was an amazing journey to freedom. You have learned the secrets of love. You have the heart of unending patience. You now see yourself as more beautiful than precious diamonds. Your relationships have been redefined with a strong bond of commitment. You are grounded on a deep and unfathomable foundation that will never crumble. You have heard Wisdom's call, and you are profoundly blessed.

You have been set free by the death and resurrection of Christ to be a woman.

Don't be discouraged by your first unsteady steps as a brand-new Bride. This redeemed life of beauty is so big and vastly uncharted. There are undiscovered paths in every place for your submissive love. Even though Wisdom has been whispering to women from the very first of creation, it takes a while to confidently hear her voice. But your dazzling wedding clothes and words of comfort will remind you of your precious place in God's story.

We will wait together for the next chapter of our story, when the long-awaited Bridegroom returns and brings a new heaven and earth.

> Then I saw a new heaven and a new earth, for the first heaven and the first earth had passed away, and the sea was no more. And I saw the holy city, new Jerusalem, coming down out of heaven from God, prepared as a bride adorned for her husband. And I heard a loud voice from the

throne saying, "Behold, the dwelling place of God is with man. He will dwell with them, and they will be his people, and God himself will be with them as their God. He will wipe away every tear from their eyes, and death shall be no more, neither shall there be mourning, nor crying, nor pain anymore, for the former things have passed away."

And he who was seated on the throne said, "Behold, I am making all things new." Also he said, "Write this down, for these words are trustworthy and true." (Revelation 21:1–5)

The old order of sin and shame, eating forbidden fruit, pain, divorce, aloneness, law, and death will be gone. Something greater had been promised back in the Garden. Something greater had silenced the power of the Evil One. Something greater is dwelling with you even now. Something greater is your eternal future.

Finally, the day will come when our story looks like what we hear. From the tragedy in the Garden to the death of our Savior, we can only wait patiently for the final celebration. Then our true story will shine like the sun. We will see our bridal gown in full splendor. Our Bridegroom will call us face to face. God will actually live with His people. Our confusion, sadness, and separation will be at a visible end.

Our promised land at the end looks very similar to the ancient Garden at the beginning. Sparkling flowing water, trees bearing fruit and life, and God and His people united in the beautiful relationship they were created for. Our end takes us right back to the beginning.

Then the angel showed me the river of the water of life, as clear as crystal, flowing from the throne of God and of the Lamb down the middle of the great street of the city. On each side of the river stood the tree of life, bearing twelve crops of fruit, yielding its fruit every month. And the leaves of the tree are for the healing of the nations. No longer will there be any curse. The throne of God and of the Lamb will be in the city, and his servants will serve him. They will see his face, and his name will be on their foreheads. There will be no more night. They will not need the light of a lamp or the light of the sun, for the Lord God will give them light. And they will reign for ever and ever. (Revelation 22:1–5)

Although hauntingly similar, this new creation is a step beyond the unmatched beauty of Eden. The blessed city is already filled with life, with a story that breathes our salvation saga. We can feel the water of life, flowing like a gentle river, washing over us, cleansing us pure and clean. We can rest in the shade of the tree of life, freed from the watchful eye of the angel's flaming sword. We can taste the sweet fruit of life, passed to us from the twelve tribes of Israel to the twelve disciples of Christ, in full bloom from the ancient Garden.

Our story returns to the first Garden, but with an obvious difference. The promise of a Savior, the prophecy of one who will crush the head of the Serpent, is gone. Now the Promised One shines in the middle of the city as the Lamb of God. Our Savior, who walked into death like a holy innocent lamb to the slaughter, now sits with the Father Almighty. God's people do what they were created to do, serve Him.

Daughter, you will finally see your long-lost home. The amazing Garden surrounds you; the gifts of life wash and feed you; the Hero of the promise stands in your midst. No longer will you struggle with the curse of pain and strife. No longer will you desire the power of your head and no longer will he rule over you. No longer will the Evil One nip at your heels. No longer will death have a part in our story. God will return to His people. You will live victorious forever more.

Wisdom has continued to tell this story time and time again. Her words carry you down the well-lit path. She calls for you to believe your story, to remember your Hero. Wisdom speaks by the angel that showed you this peaceful river of life. Wisdom washed you in baptism and marked you by the name of the Father, Son, and Holy Spirit. Wisdom has claimed you.

In the beginning, Wisdom spoke, and light appeared. In the end, Wisdom spoke that He is making all things new. The Word of Wisdom from the beginning to the end has a name: Jesus Christ.

Now that you know the end, it changes your story today. Boldly, you can live as a beautifully created woman because the end of your story is secure. Focused on your happy ending, the burden of the curse seems light. Sure of your joyful finale, the waiting and wanting and weeping is short. You are free to be a woman.

This is your story.

Further Reading

A Gift

2   **The voice created the earth**: ". . . that through His speaking God makes something out of nothing. And so here for the first time Moses mentions the means and instrument God uses in doing His work, namely, the Word." Pelikan, J., (1958), *Luther's Works, Vol. 1: Lectures on Genesis Chapters 1–5*, Saint Louis, MO: Concordia, pg. 16 (hereafter LW).

2   **She hovered there**: This story preserves the feminine article for Wisdom following the biblical metaphor in the book of Proverbs. At the same time, this story upholds the creeds to be a true confession of the Holy Trinity—three persons, one God: Father, Son, and Holy Spirit. Unlike Gnostic heresy, which elevated "Sophia" Wisdom as a separate female person of the Godhead, this story is told within the tension as it is presented in Scripture.

"While one can postulate as the basis for this female figure the idea of 'wisdom' in wisdom literature, the creation of the Sophia myth is due to an illusion of the mind rather than to an exegesis of the concept of 'wisdom.'" Brighton, L., (2008), "The Ordination of Women, a Gnostic Heresy?," *Women Pastors?*, Saint Louis, MO: Concordia, pg. 101.

2   **She loved His**: Proverbs 8:22–31. Wisdom is speaking in Proverbs about her participation in creation. "Ages ago I was . . ."

2   **A robin's small sweet song**: Genesis 1:1–19. The story of creation (All Bible verses are from the ESV unless otherwise noted).

3   **And He speaks Wisdom**: Proverbs 8:32–36. Wisdom speaks for a purpose: life.

4   **But she was always there**: Proverbs 1:1–6. The introduction to Proverbs identifies both young and old, simple and wise, as the audience for Wisdom.

4   **You will not satisfy**: Proverbs 1:7.

Dust, Life, Death

8   **Even though the newborn**: Genesis 2:18.

8   **The Lord carefully**: Genesis 2:7, 22. Man and animals were יָצַר (formed), but woman was בָּנָה (built) from already existing creation.

8   **The Lord carefully**: The Hebrew word for helper (עֵזֶר; Genesis 2:18) does not indicate a lower or "less than" role to Adam. This same word is ascribed to God in Psalms 30:11 and 54:6.

9 **"Flesh of my flesh,":** Genesis 2:23.

9 **Adam names and rules**: The exclusive task of naming creatures (including Eve) was given to Adam by God. Although God was the ultimate Creator, His work was made public by the one who named. Although both man and woman, together, would have dominion over all the animals, man was the one entrusted to speak. "In Genesis God said, 'Let there be light, and there was light.' Think about that statement logically, God named the thing before He created it; the naming seemed to be a necessary first step towards creation. Then according to Genesis, God gave man the right to name all the animals, and at the same time, the right of dominion over them." Graham, L., "The Power of Names: In Culture and in Mathematics," *Proceedings of the American Philosophical Society*, vol. 157, no. 2, June 2013, pg. 229.

9 **Adam names and rules**: Genesis 2:15. God placed man in the Garden for the purpose to work it (לְעָבְדָהּ) and for the purpose to keep it (וּלְשָׁמְרָהּ).

9 **Their special tasks**: In Genesis 1–2, both man and woman are created in God's image, neither greater in degree or worth. However, each were given distant and unique tasks as man and woman. Physical attributes that men and women still possess testify to the unique tasks each were created to do. Only women can have children based on the created body parts that define them as women. Men cannot have children, from Adam's creation to the present, and they biologically lack the physical gifts to do so. Loving dominion over creation and speaking from God are the tasks given to man, childbearing and corresponding/being a help are all distinct gifts of woman.

9 **They exist together**: "The goodness of (God's) work is never in the work itself, but only in the Creator. The goodness of the work consists precisely in the fact that it very rigidly points away from itself towards the Creator alone and to His Word which is good." Bonhoeffer, D., (1997), *Creation and Fall, Temptation; Two Biblical Studies*, New York, NY: Touchstone, pg. 36.

10 **Rather, the Serpent leads**: LW 1:146–150.

11 **She can't quite remember**: "Here the Lord is preaching to Adam and setting the word before him . . . This sermon was delivered on the sixth day; and if, as the text indicates, Adam alone heard it, he later informed Eve of it." LW 1:105.

11 **The punishment of death**: God's consequence to disobeying in 2:17 is restated by Eve in Genesis 3:3. While the command was emphatic spoken from God "you will surely die" (מוֹת תָּמוּת) Eve added "lest you will die" (פֶּן־תְּמֻתוּן) and softened the command significantly.

12 **So the next thing**: 1 Timothy 2:13–14.

12 **Daughter, today we live**: Isaiah 6:5.

12 **Likewise, we do not expect**: 1 John 1:8.

13 **The tree was given**: "But it is useful to note also that God gave Adam Word, worship, and religion in its barest, purest, and simplest form . . . Only this He wants: that he praise God, that he thank Him, that he rejoice in the Lord, and that he obey Him by not eating from the forbidden tree." LW 1:106.

14 **In fact, he made them**: "Eve falls first . . . but the culmination of the story is the fall of Adam. Eve only falls totally when Adam falls, for the two are one. Adam falls because of Eve, Eve falls because of Adam . . . Male and female He created them—and man fell away from him—male and female." Bonhoeffer, *Creation and Fall*, pg. 83.

Named

15 **The problem is this**: God demonstrated the lack of "free will" of man by forbidding the tree of the knowledge of good and evil. In other words, introducing the command not to eat shows us that Adam and Eve were never "free" from God. Luther, M., (1957), *On the Bondage of the Will*, trans. J. I. Packer and O. R. Johnston, Grand Rapids, MI: Baker Academic, pgs. 150–151.

16 **We are bound to**: "So man's will is like a beast standing between two riders. If God rides, it wills and goes where God wills . . . If Satan rides, it wills and goes where Satan wills. Nor may it choose to which rider it will run, or which it will seek; but the riders themselves fight to decide who shall have and hold it." Luther, *Bondage of the Will*, pgs. 103–104.

16 **He wants you to be less**: "Man's being *sicut deus* (as God) in fact includes his not wanting to be a creature." Bonhoeffer, *Creation and Fall*, pg. 81.

18 **Adam blames God**: LW 1:177–179.

18 **This world that**: "This is the changed, the destroyed world. At odds with God, with the other person and with nature . . ." Bonhoeffer, *Creation and Fall*, pgs. 95–96.

18 **Woman no longer rejoices**: The woman's curse is described as a "longing for the man" (וְאֶל־אִישֵׁךְ תְּשׁוּקָתֵךְ; Gen 3:16) This phrase is also used also in Genesis 4:7 where sin is "longing" for Cain (וְאֵלֶיךָ תְּשׁוּקָתוֹ; Gen 4:7) right before he kills his brother. This phrase signifies "longing" is a desire for control. For woman, part of her curse is a desire for the authority created for man. Although a good order was given by God to man and woman before the fall, the sinful world now includes her longing for control and their resulting strife.

19 **We are children**: Kolb, R., and Wengert, T., (2000), "Formula of Concord: Solid Declaration," *The Book of Concord*, Minneapolis, MN: Fortress, I.5–6, pg. 533.

19 **All have sinned**: Romans 3:23.

19 **We struggle just to live**: Gerhard, J., (1998), *Sacred Meditations*, trans. C. W. Heisler, Malone, TX: Repristination, pgs. 216–221.

21 **But now with the promise**: Genesis 3:20 "Eve" (חַוָּה) relates to the root word "life" (חיה). So Adam calls her "mother of all the living" (אֵם כָּל־חָי).

21 **Yet when this man**: "It is not God who gives her a name, it is Adam . . . he believed in life even when all nature had already been made subject to death." LW 1:219–220.

22 **Later, in a similar foreshadowing**: Leviticus 4. Sin offerings.

The Story of a Boy and a Seductress

29 **There is no escape**: Proverbs 6:32–35. The jealous husband.

30 **The angry husband**: "(St. Paul) hints at the frequent scriptural characterizations of unfaithfulness to God as adultery and this same characterization may also lie behind the father's concern in Proverbs." Steinmann, A., (2009), *Proverbs*, Saint Louis, MO: Concordia, pg. 182.

30 **He saw them**: See marriage/adultery metaphor for God's people in Ezekiel 16 and 23, 1 Corinthians 6:9–20, Galatians 5:19–25, and Ephesians 5:21–33.

30 **His hands formed**: Psalm 95.

30 **He placed each**: Psalm 139.

30 **Beasts and birds and babies**: Genesis 6:5–8.

31 **You should be scared**: ". . . Depart from me all you workers of evil, in that place there will be weeping and gnashing of teeth . . ." Luke 13:23–28.

31 This fear of His: "The fear of the Lord is the beginning of knowledge; fools despise wisdom and instruction." Proverbs 1:7.

31 You have no excuse: ". . . So they are without excuse . . ." Romans 1:16–32.

31 Fear is the beginning: Psalm 130.

32 Jesus Christ walked: The unfortunately common way of reading Proverbs *without* Christ leads to allegorization, directly relating the advice or story to modern day application. For example, "Proverbs chapter 7 is a technicolor portrait of a foolish woman. The immediate context is that of a father teaching his son how to recognize and be protected from the snare of the foolish woman. However this passage includes many insights that ought to be an indispensable part of the 'curriculum' that we as women master and pass on to the next generation of women." DeMoss, N., (2002), "Portrait of a Foolish Woman," *Biblical Womanhood in the Home*, Wheaton, IL: Crossway Books, pg. 85.

However, in employing a Christological hermeneutic, Christ is at the center and is the focus of every interpretation, especially regarding righteousness.

33 He waited for: Luther, M., (1957), *Christian Liberty*, ed. H. J. Grimm, Philadelphia, PA: Fortress, pg. 15.

33 He paid the death toll: "The Son of God came down from heaven to choose His bride from among men condemned and devoted to eternal death. The whole race to which the bride belonged was hostile to the heavenly father, but He reconciled it to His Father by His most bitter passion." Gerhard, *Sacred Meditations*, pg. 73.

34 In fear of our awesome: "Thus 'the fear of Yahweh' is first and foremost a filial relationship initiated by God when He reckons sinners as righteous through faith (Gen 15:6, Is. 53:11, Hab. 2:4)." Steinmann, "The Fear of Yahweh," *Proverbs*, pgs. 27–28.

34 We are wise: "Wisdom is inseparable from righteousness. When given divine advice and teaching, the wise and righteous person grows in learning, and this learning is predicated on the fear of Yahweh. The salvific fear includes not only dread of God's wrath at sin according to His Law, but also faith in God as Savior and love for God." Steinmann, *Proverbs*, pg. 29.

34 By no merit: "By the wedding ring of faith he shares in the sins, death, and pains of hell which are his bride's. As a matter of fact, he makes them his own and acts as if they were his own and as if he himself had sinned; he suffered, died and descended into hell that he might overcome them all." Luther, *Christian Liberty*, pg. 15.

Personal Truth

35 But here your personal: "All proper application of sacred scripture involves theological interpretation of its texts . . . We are not to see how we/our people 'fit into the story.' Rather the reality of which we are a part—indeed the reality which has seized us—is the same reality which invaded our world decisively in the OT and, especially, in NT times. It is for this reason that these texts may and must be applied to us to us today." Voelz, J. W., (1997), *What Does This Mean?*, Saint Louis, MO: Concordia, pg. 341.

36 Wisdom did not forget: "The parallelism 'earth . . . heavens' (Proverbs 3:19) recalls Genesis 1:1 and makes Wisdom an active participant in creation. This identifies Wisdom as Christ, by whom all things were made (John 1:3, Colossians 1:16)" Steinmann, *Proverbs*, pg. 119.

38 Experience was born: "This is all the old devil and old snake, who also turned Adam and Eve into enthusiasts and led them from the external Word of God to 'spirituality' and their own presumption." "Smalcald Articles," *Book of Concord*, VIII.5, pg. 322.

38 Wisdom tells a story: "Furthermore, to put aside all kinds of works, even contempla-
tion, meditation, and all that the soul can do, does not help. One thing, and the only
thing, is necessary for Christian life, righteousness, and freedom. That one thing is the
most holy Word of God, the gospel of Christ." Luther, *Christian Liberty*, pg. 8.

41 Our experiences can lead: The implied "reader" of the Bible interprets within the
Christian community with "other readers, with other receptors, with those who are her
contemporaries, and with those who have gone before." So it follows that the proper
interpretation of scripture flows from the ancient creeds, embraces the Christian faith
(believes), and focuses on Christ as the center (Christocentric). Voelz, *What Does This
Mean?*, pgs. 217–229.

41 He is the one: "And the Lord said to Job: 'Shall a faultfinder contend with the Almighty?
He who argues with God, let him answer it.' Then Job answered the Lord and said,
'Behold, I am of small account; what shall I answer you? I lay my hand on my mouth.'"
Job 40:1–4.

Shadows of Independence

43 Even my own beloved: *The Service of Women in Congregational and Synodical
Offices: A Report of the Commission on Theology and Church Relations of the Lutheran
Church—Missouri Synod*, (2005), Saint Louis, MO: Concordia.

45 From the earliest beginning: "Our creation as male and female therefore tells us that
'we are created not for life in isolation but for community, a community which binds
those who are different.' God's 'very good' work of human creation continues to be
seen in this beautiful fact that from the beginning, we are made not to stand alone, but
together. As individuals, we were made not to be isolated tangled threads, but to be
part of a divine tapestry reflecting His beautiful design." *Creator's Tapestry: A Report of
the Commission on Theology and Church Relations of the Lutheran Church—Missouri
Synod*, (2009), Saint Louis, MO: Concordia, pg. 42.

45 We are told: "Our mission is to offer assistance to those in need, provide the necessary
tools to become free, socially, financially, spiritually and mentally . . . Our programs
will re-engage women in the employment sector, help them broaden their horizons
through peer counseling and most importantly become *self-sufficient* (emphasis mine)."
Truly Liberated Women home page, retrieved May 3, 2017, http://www.trulyliberated
.org.

45 We mindlessly encourage: "You Are the Creator of Your Life! / This is your Power, This
is your birth right / Life isn't about finding yourself it's about / Creating Yourself!" The
Liberated Women home page, retrieved May 3, 2017, http://www.theliberatedwomen
.com.

"I am free, I have the last say over what I believe as an adult. The only beliefs that
I entertain are those that are self-nurturing . . . I choose to believe in myself, even
during challenging times. My sense of self is anchored in my knowledge that I am
worthy of love and success. It comes from within." The Liberated Woman in Life, "I
Have Freed Myself from Self-Limiting Beliefs," The Liberated Women, October 11,
2014, https:// theliberatedwomen .wordpress .com/ 2014/ 10/ 11/ i -have -freed -myself
-from-self-limiting-beliefs/.

46 He clothes us all: Galatians 3:27, Ephesians 4:24, and Isaiah 61:10. Clothed in
righteousness.

46 **This describes our true freedom**: "Galatians 3:28 is the text most frequently cited by the woman's ordination movement. (But) the topic is the baptismal identity of all believers in Christ Jesus. The verse must be read in context . . . Ordination is another topic which Paul addresses elsewhere." Lockwood, G., (2000), *1 Corinthians*, Saint Louis, MO: Concordia, pgs. 535–536.

47 **A "freedom" from God**: "Frequently it is concluded at this point that between all members of the church there must exist complete similarity. People are of the opinion that in these words we find a different, in fact, a more genuine basic New Testament stance than, for instance, in 1 Corinthians 14:34. However that is to tear the words from their context and to give them a meaning they do not have. For in Gal. 3:28, we are speaking of the unity of Christ (all are one). This unity, which finds its basis in baptism (v. 27), is realized in fellowship with Christ, where, despite the most extreme outward differences, we form an indissoluble unity. Therefore the New Testament here emphasizes, as in other passages, these two: unity and diversity." Giertz, B., (2008), "Twenty Three Theses on the Holy Scriptures, the Woman, and the Office of the Ministry," *Women Pastors?*, Saint Louis, MO: Concordia, pg. 175.

47 **Because they are His creatures**: "(Adam) was so created that as long as he lived in this physical life he would till the ground, not as if he were doing an irksome task and exhausting his body by toil but with supreme pleasure; not as a pastime but in obedience to God and submission to His will." LW 1:65.

47 **God was the head**: "Instead of independence, the ideal is dependence . . . Thus Paul asks us to submit joyfully to those whom the Father has given to care for us." Winger, T. M., (2015), *Ephesians*, Saint Louis, MO: Concordia, pgs. 641–642.

47 **Where he should have stood**: "It was something serious to turn away from God and from His Word . . . but what is something far more serious now happens: that Eve agrees with Satan when he charges God with lying." LW 1:156.

47 **Whether he acted out**: "Therefore, just as sin came into the world through one man, and death through sin, and so death spread to all men because all sinned . . ." Romans 5:12.

48 **Instead of love**: "The Large Catechism, the First Part: The Ten Commandments," *Book of Concord*, 1–29, pgs. 386–390.

48 **We saw Him walk**: Koester, C. R., (1995), *Symbolism in the Fourth Gospel*, Minneapolis, MN: Fortress, pg. 75, 115–118.

48 **Some of us are torn**: The other side of the spectrum—"No woman can call herself free who does not control her own body." Sanger, M., Women's Right to Choose home page, retrieved May 3, 2017, http://www.womensrighttochoose.weebly.com.

48 **Some of us are pulled**: One side of the spectrum, Christians commonly use the "Proverbs 31 woman" as a model of righteousness. They will go so far as to withdraw a list of biblical principles to determine if a woman is acting submissive or not. "The woman of virtue portrayed in Proverbs 31 is commended for watching over the affairs of her household . . . it is the woman's responsibility to be the caretaker for the home. Domesticity—devotion to the quality of home life—is an essential facet of femininity." Mahaney, C., (2002), "Femininity," *Biblical Womanhood in the Home*, Wheaton, IL: Crossway Books, pg. 29.

In the end, this view binds the heart's compliance to God's law, ignores our failure to complete that law, and overshadows the truth of the Gospel—a righteousness that is from Christ alone.

49 **I am bound to another**: Luther, *Christian Liberty*, pgs. 14–15.

49 He submitted to death: "He humbled himself by becoming obedient to death—even death on a cross!" Philippians 2:8.

Submission in the Muddy Water

50 When the world fights: ". . . the wife owns whatever belongs to the husband. Hence all of us who believe in Christ are priests and kings in Christ." Luther, *Christian Liberty*, pg. 17.

51 He asked only one thing: Exodus 20. "Let us, then, learn well the First Commandment, that we may see how God will tolerate no presumption nor any trust in any other object, and how He requires nothing higher of us than confidence from the heart for everything good . . . Let this suffice with respect to the First Commandment, which we have had to explain at length, since it is of chief importance, because, as before said, where the heart is rightly disposed toward God and this commandment is observed, all the others follow." Luther, M., *The Book of Concord: The Large Catechism*, retrieved May 8, 2017, http://bookofconcord.org/lc-3-tencommandments.php.

51 Much later, a tiny baby: John 1:1–15.

51 Even when Jesus prayed: John 17.

52 Among other things: "Because the Ephesian Christians have become enlightened through Christ's shining upon them in Holy Baptism (5:14; cf. 1:18, 4:5) they are now able to see clearly how they should walk (5:15). Concretely, this means that God's Word has made them 'wise' (5:15), and by the continual application of that Word they will be able to see what they should believe and do." Winger, *Ephesians*, pg. 593.

53 There in the water: "(Jesus) begins his substitutionary atonement by condescending to take his place among sinners submitting to a baptism of repentance." Just, A. A., (1996), *Luke 1:1–9:50*, Saint Louis, MO: Concordia, pg. 161.

53 And Jesus perfectly submitted: "Subordination in nature has been placed there by God not to indicate that someone is more worthy than another or that one should be despised. Subordination is for the sake of function and welfare. The child is subordinate to the parents for the child's welfare, not to punish the child or to benefit the parents. Christ is subordinate to God in carrying out the task of salvation. This does not degrade Christ. The church is subordinate to Christ. The one in the superior or upper position exercises love to those in the lower positions." Scaer, D., (2008), "May Women Be Ordained as Pastors?," *Women Pastors?*, Saint Louis, MO: Concordia, pg. 247.

53 Submission is what Christ: "Christ is not only represented by earthly parents, to whom children submit, but Christ is also the perfect Son, who models true submission and forgives the failure to conform to his model." Winger, *Ephesians*, pg. 673.

53 Paul describes Christians: Ὑποτασσόμενοι ἀλλήλοις (*being subordinate to one another*; Ephesians 5:21). This is the third participle clause, which is dependent on the imperative πληροῦσθε ἐν πνεύματι (*be filled up with the Spirit*; Ephesians 5:18).

"Willing subordination to one another within the body of Christ is first a gift of the Spirit, from which a second series of consequences may be derived. The clause is therefore a hinge connecting the work of the Spirit (5:18–20) to the entire 'household table' that follows (5:21–6:9)." Winger, *Ephesians*, pg. 599.

53 It is weaved: "Subordination is, first, built into creation itself." Winger, *Ephesians*, pg. 642.

53 A Christian woman gives: "Being subordinate is therefore not only 'taking one's place in the order,' but also recognizing Christ in the person placed above." Winger, *Ephesians*, pg. 630.

54 **And this is how a Christian**: "For each day as the husband loves his wife in a thor-
    oughly self-sacrificing way, he proclaims Jesus Christ to her . . . And each day as she
    submits to his love, as she entrusts herself to him, as she respects his headship, she . . .
    sees the contours of Christ's redeeming sacrifice in the Christlike figure God has
    placed into her life" (Luther's second wedding sermon on Ephesians 5:22–33). Winger,
    Ephesians, pg. 653.

55 **She is a new creation**: Koester, *Symbolism in the Fourth Gospel*, pg. 184.

56 **We feel His care**: "Behold, thus God wishes to indicate to us how He cares for us in all
    our need, and faithfully provides also for our temporal support. And although He abun-
    dantly grants and preserves these things even to the wicked and knaves, yet He wishes that
    we pray for them, in order that we may recognize that we receive them from His hand,
    and may feel His paternal goodness toward us therein. For when He withdraws His hand,
    nothing can prosper nor be maintained in the end, as, indeed, we daily see and experi-
    ence." Luther, "Lord's Prayer," *Large Catechism*, pgs. 82–83.

Gong and Cymbal

59 **Bountifully displayed before**: "So then this tree of the knowledge of good and evil,
    or the place where trees of this kind were planted in large number, would have been
    the church at which Adam, together with his descendants, would have gathered on the
    Sabbath day . . . Only this (God) wants that (Adam) praise God, that he thank Him,
    that he rejoice in the Lord, and that He obey by not eating of the forbidden tree." LW
    1:106.

59 **As we remember**: Luther speaks of the image of God ascribed to Adam, but in this case
    also Eve. "Therefore my understanding of the image of God is this: that Adam had it in
    his being and that he not only knew God and believed that He was good, but that he
    also lived a life that was wholly godly; that is, he was without fear of death or any other
    danger, and was content with God's favor." LW 1:63.

60 **Even with the bright light**: John 1:5.

60 **Love behaves kindly**: "Whereas English translations generally resort to adjectives in
    translating many of these verbs, the Greek has a dynamic quality well suited to the
    way love expresses itself *in actions* for the benefit of others." Lockwood, *1 Corinthians*,
    pg. 464.

61 **But we are all part**: "Instead of nurturing divisiveness, the various parts of the organ-
    ism should be anxiously and thoughtfully concerned about one another (1 Corinthians
    12:25) . . . Paul is laying the groundwork for 1 Corinthians 13, his great chapter on
    love." Lockwood, *1 Corinthians*, pg. 448.

61 **Sharing these gifts**: "Love is to be the all-dominating motive in seeking and in using
    spiritual gifts." Lenski, R. C. H., (1998), *The Interpretation of St. Paul's First and Second
    Epistles to the Corinthians*, Peabody, MA: Hendrickson, pg. 543.

61 **The gift of tongues**: Lockwood, *1 Corinthians*, pgs. 484–487.

63 **Rather, as the Old Testament says**: Lenski, *1–2 Corinthians*, pg. 616.

63 **This chapter speaks**: Paul uses the verb "to speak" (λαλεῖν) in the verses about both
    gift of speaking in tongues (1 Corinthians 14:5, 39) and gift of speaking as a woman
    (1 Corinthians 14:34, 35). In both cases these gifts are good and from God. However,
    these particular gifts are also restrained in the public worship setting.

63 **It is not just disgraceful**: "Paul has no modifier with αἰσχρὸν 'shameful.' The term does
    imply that the act mentioned is shameful, highly improper, in someone's judgment.

The only judge who Paul has appealed in this entire connection is 'the Law,' the Divine Word, and thus God Himself." Lenski, *1–2 Corinthians*, pg. 619.

66 **Punished for our knowledge**: "How can the Lord impute our iniquities to us after He hath once imputed to another? For the sins of the people he hath smitten His dearly beloved Son." Gerhard, *Sacred Meditations*, pg. 56.

67 **First, women wear good deeds**: "Paul says they should learn 'quietly' (ἐν ἡσυχίᾳ) Most scholars today argue that this word does not actually mean 'silence' here but refers to a quiet demeanor and a spirit that is peaceable instead of argumentative." Schreiner, T., (2016), "A Dialogue with Scholarship," *Women in the Church*, Wheaton, IL: Crossway Books, pg. 186.

67 **Third, women do not**: Ancient literature uses the word αὐθεντεῖν (1 Timothy 2:12) to mean "the active use of authority." "Therefore, 'to exercise authority' in the sense of ruling, controlling, or dominating without inherently possessing the authority to do so appears to be what Paul is signifying with his use of this term." Gieschen, "Ordained Proclaimers or Quiet Learners?," *Women Pastors?*, pg. 81.

67 **Lest we believe**: ἐπιτρέπω (to permit) is the subject of some controversy that is said to reflect a temporary, time-bound prohibition. But Paul has used this form of the verb (present indicative) for universal commands in other places. Schreiner, "A Dialogue with Scholarship," *Women in the Church*, pg. 189.

67 **Lest we believe**: "The passive form of the verb ἐπιτρέπω 'to permit,' in the phrase 'it is not permitted' (οὐ ἐπιτρέπεται, 14:34) indicates that God is behind the command . . . Behind the apostle's word (cf. 1 Timothy 2:12; 'I do not permit a woman to teach') stands the word of God." Lockwood, *1 Corinthians*, pg. 508.

67 **St. Paul grounds his words**: "In v. 13, then, the causal γαρ strengthens Paul's directions by appealing to the Genesis creation account, and the connective και opening v. 14 adds a second observation regarding Adam: not only was he created first (v. 13), but he was also not deceived (the woman was, δε). While v. 14 contrasts Adam and Eve, the connective δε (rather than αλλα) juxtaposes the two assertions in v. 14 regarding Adam and Eve as distinct points." Kostenberger, A., (2016), "A Complex Sentence," *Women in the Church*, Wheaton, IL: Crossway Books, pg. 157.

68 **First in God's**: "The Christian family under the husband's headship forms the pattern for the Christian congregation . . . According to his sketch in 1 Timothy of the creation account, the woman has a subordinate role both before and after the fall." Lockwood, *1 Corinthians*, pg. 509.

68 **Adam was created**: Even in the realm of mathematics, the authority of the namer is recognized. Adam was given that specific gift in his creation as man, which is also manifested in the life of the church today. "A common concept in history is that knowing the name of something or someone gives one power over that thing or person. This concept occurs in many different forms in numerous cultures." "Mathematicians occasionally observe that, on the basis of intuition, they sometimes develop concepts that are at first ineffable and resist definition; these concepts must be named before they can be brought under control and properly enter the mathematical world. Naming can be the path toward that control." Graham, "The Power of Names," *Proceedings of the American Philosophical Society*, pg. 229, 231.

68 **And she most certainly forgot**: "In approaching Eve, then, the Serpent subverted the pattern of male leadership and interacted only with the woman. Adam was present throughout and did not intervene. The Genesis temptation, therefore stands as the

prototype of what happens when male leadership is abrogated." Schreiner, "A Dialogue with Scholarship," *Women in the Church*, pg. 215.

68 Man is still created: "The Church organically relates to such preaching and teaching as that which is created by and through such speaking. In short, the Church is constituted in the hearing of faith which arises out of such authoritative speaking. And this fact I would like to argue, possesses a substantive and organic relation to the relational order of man and woman given in creation." Weinrich, W., (2008), "It Is Not Given to Women to Teach," *Women Pastors?*, Saint Louis, MO: Concordia, pg. 367.

68 The identity of man: "The proscription on women teaching men, then stems not from the fall and cannot be ascribed to the curse. Paul appeals to the created order, the good and perfect world God made, to justify the ban on women teaching men." Schreiner, "A Dialogue with Scholarship," *Women in the Church*, pg. 199–200.

69 This childbirth will save: "Yet woman we are told, 'will be saved by childbearing,' in the course of which Christ became born of a woman." Gorday, P., ed., (2000), *Ancient Christian Commentary on Scripture, New Testament, Vol. 9*, Downers Grove, IL: InterVarsity Press, pg. 166.

69 This Child was: "When Paul says that women will be saved by childbearing, he means, therefore, that they will be saved by adhering to their ordained role . . . Since Paul elsewhere argues that salvation is gained not on the basis of our works, I think it is fair to understand the virtues described here as a result of new life in Christ." Schreiner, "A Dialogue with Scholarship," *Women in the Church*, pgs. 222–223.

70 If you focus your own: "Therefore, faith is a constant gaze that looks at nothing except Christ, the Victor over sin and death and the Dispenser of righteousness, salvation, and eternal life. In his epistles, therefore, Paul sets forth and urges Jesus Christ in almost every verse." LW 26:356.

70 You cannot by your own reason: "Small Catechism: The Creed, The Third Article," *Book of Concord*, pg. 355.

70 Our submissive love: "The redemption accomplished by Christ restored the fallen creation, including the gender distinctiveness of male and female; it does not change the basic nature of creation." Gieschen, "Ordained Proclaimers or Quiet Learners?," *Woman Pastors?*, pg. 84.

70 He always protects: 1 Corinthians 13:4–8.

Top-Down Organization

74 He praises his brothers: Commending the Corinthians for passing on traditions. Lockwood, *1 Corinthians*, pg. 361.

74 This is the greater truth: "From the outset, it should be noted that Paul does not wish to set in concrete a rule *about specific practices* for all places and times regarding head-coverings. (When he does state a universal and permanent rule for practice, he often refers to a direct command from God, as in 14:37 . . .) Rather he is establishing the *universal and permanent principal* that men and woman at worship should conduct themselves modestly and sensibly in keeping with whatever happen to be the customs of the time." Lockwood, *1 Corinthians*, pg. 362.

74 They were already doing: "The Corinthians are in accord with Paul in regard to this question. What he has taught them regarding the position and the conduct of women is still in force among them." Lenski, *1–2 Corinthians*, pg. 430.

74 **The following discussion**: ". . . Paul is not laying down an absolute rule that is to be observed by Christians of all times in regard to covering the head or leaving it uncovered during worship. Not the custom as a custom is vital but the *significance* of a custom." Lenski, *1–2 Corinthians*, pg. 435.

75 **Although it could seem**: Scholars debate over the praying and prophesy of women here in 1 Corinthians 11:5 and Paul's contradictory words in 1 Corinthians 14:35: "it is shameful for a woman to speak in church." "Paul's approach, then, is a fine example of wise pastoral care. Not everything can be addressed at once. A foundation must first be laid before the more difficult things that must be said can be said. Thus Paul in 11:2–16 is not yet ready to issue 'the Lord's command' (14:37) regarding women. He restricts himself primarily to the issue of their head-coverings and prayer." (See also chapters 8 and 10 on meals in pagan temples.) Lockwood, *1 Corinthians*, pg. 534.

75 **A woman praying**: "A new kind of woman appears precisely at the time of Cicero and Caesar; a woman in high position, who nevertheless claims for herself the indulgence in sexuality of a woman of pleasure." "For a Christian wife to indicate that she placed herself among the high class 'new' Roman women grossly misrepresented the teaching of Christianity on marriage." Winter, B. W., (2001), *After Paul Left Corinth*, Grand Rapids, MI: William B. Eerdmans, pg. 123, 129.

75 **She publicly humiliated**: "And the same Word of God is addressed to all. From one point of view, indeed there are two horizons . . . from the divine perspective, there is really only one horizon." Lockwood, *1 Corinthians*, pg. 522.

75 **These words also speak**: The significance of this text is found in a theological connection to other verses explored previously about the order of Christ, men and women. "If one is interpreting matrices of things, events, situations, etc., the second question is, 'What significance may be given to items which are portrayed or presented in a text?' In general, the 'significance' will either be cultural or theological . . . it is generally true that the theological significances are of greater concern. Theological significance is chiefly understood with respect to God both his nature and his relationship to us, but also with respect to humanity, both our nature and, especially, our relationship with God." Voelz, *What Does This Mean?*, pg. 161.

75 **In our story even today**: "1 Corinthians 11:10 employs metonymy with the word 'authority.' 'Which complex characteristics does one actually intend to evoke and which referent has characteristics which correspond to it?' . . . The conceptual signified evoked by this signifier cannot be that intended, since one does not have power itself on one's head, rather, some symbol of power." Voelz, *What Does This Mean?*, pg. 171.

76 **Headcovering is a visual display**: "Because the relationship between man and woman has the nature of a kephale-structure, the position of each in its created existence differs from that of the other for all time. Their positions cannot be interchanged. The original creaturely 'from' and 'for the sake of' relates to the woman; the reverse is not possible!" Brunner, P., (2008), "The Ministry and the Ministry of Women," *Women Pastors?*, Saint Louis, MO: Concordia, pg. 205.

76 **They are given these gifts**: "This becoming one is never the fusion of the two, the abolition of their creatureliness as individuals. It is the utmost possible realization of their belonging to one another, which is based directly upon the fact that they are different from one another." Bonhoeffer, *Creation and Fall*, pg. 65.

76 **Man was given**: "Neither can exist without the other. There is full equality 'in the Lord' (1:11) created by baptismal unity of male and female in Christ (Gal 3:28)." Lockwood, *1 Corinthians*, pg. 375.

76 Man and woman need: Some assert that the defining story of man and woman is found in Genesis 1:27–28. "Male and female he created *them*," as proof that there was an equality in task and authority. "In a more concrete manner, Genesis 2 reiterates the message of chapter 1 . . . Their similar tasks necessitate the work of equals. Eve and Adam are equal in rank, equal in image. Genesis 2, like Genesis 1 declares and explains male and female equality, joint rulership, and interrelationship . . . God's image needs male and female to reflect God more fully." Spencer, A., (1985), *Beyond the Curse*, Nashville, TN: Thomas Nelson, pg. 28–29.

This places a singular focus on the Genesis 1 account and unnaturally shifts the force of the other biblical creation accounts, especially those interpreted in the New Testament. Rather, reading both Genesis 1 and 2 while acknowledging their different perspectives is preferable. Genesis 1 is considering the larger picture of creation, the "forest," including one-flesh man and woman created in the image of God. Genesis 2 is a closer look at the details, the "trees," the intricate development of God's man and woman, their disobedience, and their salvation. Therefore, both are true and accurate accounts, interpreted soundly by the New Testament apostles and early church.

78 Likewise, men who have long hair: Lockwood, *1 Corinthians*, pgs. 377–378.

79 There is not one: "Just as people who are bodily dead cannot on the basis of their own power prepare themselves or dispose themselves to receive temporal life once again, so people who are spiritually dead in sins cannot on the basis of their own strength dispose themselves or turn themselves toward appropriate spiritual heavenly righteousness and life, if the Son of God has not made them alive and freed them from the death of sin." "Solid Declaration," *Book of Concord*, II.11, pg. 545.

79 What she is wearing matters: Isaiah 61:10.

79 On account of Christ:

> "The gifts Christ freely gives He give to you and me.
> To be his Church, His bride, His chosen, saved and free!
> Saints blest with these rich gifts are children who proclaim.
> That they were won by Christ and cling to His strong name."

"The Gifts Christ Freely Gives," *Lutheran Service Book*, (2006), Saint Louis, MO: Concordia, pg. 602.

79 Because the practice: The word "custom" (συνήθειαν; 1Co 11:16) refers to the tradition of headcovering in the Corinthian church. "Regardless of culture, the customs and practices derived from the culture and used in the worshipping congregation should reflect and never go against divinely established principle. The principle is that the man is the head of woman, as Christ is the head of man. But note in this section that Paul is not setting down an eternal binding custom." Scaer, D., "May Women Be Ordained as Pastors?," *Women Pastors?*, pg. 241.

80 We are dead: "How then should Sunday and other similar church ordinances and ceremonies be regarded? Our people reply that bishops and pastors may make regulations for the sake of good order in the church, but not thereby to obtain God's grace, to make satisfaction for sin, or to bind consciences, nor to regard such as a service of God or to consider it a sin when these rules are broken without giving offense." "Augsburg Confession," *Book of Concord*, XXVIII.53, pg. 98.

The Groaning

84   **He encourages us**: According to the full context of 1 Peter 2:18, "Subjection to the masters is the part of Christian slaves, not a subjection like that of pagan slaves, which is due to mere human compulsion, but one that is due to submission to God's will." Lenski, R. C. H., (1998), *The Interpretation of the Epistles of St. Peter, St. John, and St. Jude*, Peabody, MA: Hendrickson, pg. 115.

85   **Her stomach twisted**: Genesis 20.

85   **She expected Him to care**: Genesis 17:15–21.

85   **She believed this story**: Luke 1:38.

86   **You, my daughter**: Romans 8:31–39.

86   **Christ has loved you**: Psalm 23.

86   **At the very same time**: 1 Corinthians 15:57.

87   **For this you have been called**: "For this and all of us are called to suffer and to be abused while we as followers of Christ conscientiously do good to others . . . From start to finish Peter presents Jesus, our example, as our Savior, who, by becoming our example, also enables us to follow his example by ridding us of our sins by bearing them for us and thus placing us into a new life." Lenski, *Epistles of St. Peter*, pg. 199.

87   **Other false teachers**: "A theology of glory calls evil good and good evil. A theology of the cross calls the thing what it actually is. This is clear: He who does not know Christ does not know God hidden in suffering. Therefore he prefers, works to suffering, glory to the cross, strength to weakness, wisdom to folly, and, in general, good to evil. These are the people whom the apostle calls 'enemies of the cross of Christ' (Phil. 3:18), for they hate the cross and suffering and love works and the glory of works. Thus they call the good of the cross evil and the evil of a deed good" (Martin Luther, "Heidelberg Disputation," 1518). LW 31:53.

87   **Rather, our life joined**: "There is reserved for the Christian a suffering of which the world knows nothing: suffering for the sake of the Lord Jesus Christ (1 Peter 4:12, 17). This suffering, too, happens to him as temptation . . . That the righteous man suffers on account of his sin is understandable; but that the righteous man suffers for the sake of righteousness, that can easily lead him to the stumbling-block in Jesus Christ." Bonhoeffer, D., (1997), *Creation and Fall, Temptation: Two Biblical Studies*, New York, NY: Touchstone, pg. 136.

88   **Back in Ephesians**: Ephesians 5:25–33.

89   **Yet these days**: "In a manner reminiscent of the OT psalms (e.g., Pss 65:12–13, 98:4–9, 148:1–14) Paul personifies creation. Throughout (Romans) 8:19–22 'creation' refers to all God has made, including all of humanity." Middendorf, M. P., (2013), *Romans 1–8*, Saint Louis, MO: Concordia, pg. 669.

89   **And we live right**: "The baptized believer's release from slavery to sin, the dominion of death, and the lordship of the Law has not ended conflict, but, rather, has inaugurated the struggle that is the Christian life." Middendorf, *Romans*, pg. 677.

89   **It is just who we are**: Psalm 46.

Confidently Ever After

92   **God will actually live**: "Here in Revelation 21 John sees the end result of the redemption of the bride of God, now spoken of as the bride of Christ. In all her godly beauty, as portrayed by the holy city Jerusalem, she will forever remain in God's holy presence." Brighton, L. A., (1999), *Revelation*, Saint Louis, MO: Concordia, pg. 596.

92 Sparkling flowing water: "The vision in this passage is also derived, significantly, from the representation of the first Eden in Gen 2, where a river flows out of the Garden (2:10), and gold and precious stones belong to one of its tributaries (verses 11–12)." Smalley, S., (2005), *The Revelation to John*, Downers Grove, IL: InterVarsity Press, pg. 561.

"In Rev 22:1–5 John sees another depiction of the new heaven and earth, this time reminiscent of the Garden of Eden. Though Eden itself is not explicitly mentioned, 'the river of the water of life' (22:1) and especially 'the tree of life' (22:2) are obvious allusions to the primeval paradise." Brighton, *Revelation*, pg. 623.

93 Wisdom washed you: "But with the Word of God it is a baptism, that is, a grace filled water of life and a 'bath of the new birth in the Holy Spirit' as St. Paul says to Titus in chapter 3(:5–8), 'through the bath of rebirth and renewal of the Holy Spirit, which he richly poured out over us through Jesus Christ our Savior, so that through that very grace we may be righteous and heirs in hope of eternal life.'" "Small Catechism: The Sacrament of Holy Baptism," *Book of Concord*, (10), pg. 359.

93 In the end, Wisdom spoke: Revelation 21:5. "It is a creative word, a spoken word by which God creates. In Genesis 1 several times it is written, 'And God said.' After each 'And God said' there follows the word he actually spoke: 'Let there be light' (Gen 1:3) ... By these words God created in each case what his words described." Brighton, *Revelation*, pg. 600.

93 Sure of your joyful finale: "To see God—ah! That will surpass all the joys of earth. To gaze on the face of Christ, to live with Christ, to hear the voice of Christ, will far exceed the most ardent desires of our hearts. O Lord Jesus, Thou most blessed Spouse of my soul, when wilt Thou bring my soul into Thy royal palace as Thine honored bride? What can I want there that Thou wilt not supply? What more can we desire or look for when God himself shall be all in all? ... There our hopes will become blissful reality. There we shall not simply sojourn, but we shall dwell in a secure abode forever and ever!" Gerhard, *Sacred Meditations*, pg. 275, 278.

CPSIA information can be obtained
at www.ICGtesting.com
Printed in the USA
LVOW08s0041050817

543752LV00007B/18/P